LAUGH

40 Women Humorists

OUT

Celebrate Then and Now

LOUD

...Before We Forget

LAUGH

40 Women Humorists

OUT

Celebrate Then and Now

LOUD

...Before We Forget

By Allia Zobel Nolan

with contributions from the Erma Bombeck
Writers' Workshop Authors

*Laugh Out Loud: 40 Women Humorists Celebrate Then and Now
...Before We Forget*

This title is also available as an ebook.

In association with the Erma Bombeck Writers' Workshop and the
University of Dayton

ISBN-13: 978-0692076194
ISBN-10: 0692076190

Cover design: Mary pat Pino
Interior design and production: Marshelle Williams

What People Are Saying about *Laugh Out Loud*

"When I was 75, I wrote *The Smartest Woman I Know*. It's not about me. But after writing five bestsellers, I'm smart enough to know the recipe for living well and enjoying it more is a good laugh. In *Laugh Out Loud*, 40 funny ladies share their wit in a book of short, hysterical, anecdotal stories you can dip in and out of on occasion, for instance, in the recovery room after a colonoscopy, or to help quell the pain of a lip wax. It lives up to its title: you'll laugh out loud."

> –Author of five bestsellers, Ilene (Gingy)
> Beckerman, wrote her first book at 60: *Love,
> Loss and What I Wore. The New York Times
> Book Review* described it as "a gem of a book
> worthy of a Tiffany Box." The book became a hit
> Off-Broadway play.

"Want to avoid wrinkles, stay svelte, and invest smart? This book can't help. But if you're looking for an irreverent, non-soppy, laugh-until-you-gag reminder that the only way to survive and thrive in life is to hang on to your sense of humor, then *Laugh Out Loud* is just the ticket. Just don't read it with a mouthful of coffee."

> –Kathy Kinney and Cindy Ratzlaff, Authors,
> *Queen of Your Own Life: The Grown-up Woman's
> Guide to Claiming Happiness and Getting the Life
> You Deserve*

"We need to adopt a philosophy of living a joyous life every day...not just on holidays or special occasions. This is the best buffer against stress that I know of. And what better way to get in a positive mood than to include a healthy dose of daily laughter? That's where *Laugh Out Loud* comes in. The stories in this side-splitting collection will have stress on the run as you nod in agreement and laugh until you can't breathe."

> —Loretta LaRoche, TV personality, Emmy Award
> nominee, bestselling author of eight books,
> founder of The Humor Potential, Inc.,
> international stress expert and creator of the
> "Love, Laughter and Lasagna" program.

"My mother would have loved *Laugh Out Loud*. It's the kind of collection that honors her sense of the ridiculous and shines a brilliant spotlight on the inane. The stories in this book reflect a philosophy she always believed: "If you can't make it better, you can laugh at it."

> —Betsy Bombeck, daughter of
> humorist Erma Bombeck

"In the spirit of Erma Bombeck, one of the greatest humorists of all time, this collection celebrates the voice of women who are smart, strong, and funny! From yoga poses to funeral arrangements to dating mishaps, these stories will not only entertain, but also remind us that life is too short not to laugh!"

> —Lisa Scottoline and Francesca Serritella,
> *New York Times* bestselling authors of
> *I See Life Through Rose-Colored Glasses*

What's Inside

Then

and...Now

Dedication

For God, who imbued me with an insatiable urge to tell funny stories that make people smile; for my husband, Desmond Finbarr Nolan, who has supported my writing addiction and never once, (as close relatives have in the past), encouraged me to "get a real job"; and for Erma Bombeck, my hero, who took the art of women's humor to the nth degree by suggesting that the "perfect woman" was really a myth and that there was more fun in serving cold pizza for breakfast, avoiding ironing pillow cases, and using dust to protect the furniture than we ever imagined; for Erma's husband, Bill Bombeck, who went to be with his wife in January 2018, and, finally, for readers everywhere who believe the best way to go through life is to throw your head back, open your mouth, and from the bottom of your belly, laugh out loud.

—ALLIA ZOBEL NOLAN

Acknowledgements

This book would never have seen the light of day, or be subject to the whims of my cats pushing it off my desk to get my attention, without the encouragement, help, support, patience, and dogged perseverance of Teri Rizvi, founder and director of the Erma Bombeck Writers' Workshop, and her Humor Anthology Team. Extreme thanks is also proffered to the extraordinarily talented funny ladies who saw fit to join me in this project by sharing their most entertaining and poignant stories. I raise my Erma mug to salute and thank them all profusely. Thanks also to creative director, Mary pat Pino, for her endless patience during the long and winding road to a cover. And finally, to Marshelle Williams for her sterling design and production of the book under a neck-breaking deadline.

—AZN

"When humor goes, there goes civilization."

—ERMA BOMBECK

Introduction

Those of us of a certain age have a storehouse of memories reflecting (pardon the idiom) "the way we were."

We ironed our hair and rolled it in soda cans. We slathered on cement-colored lipstick that turned us into zombie princesses. We used Dippity-Do, Aqua Net, and wore perfume that made us smell like lemons. We openly idolized people like Twiggy, yet secretly wanted to be Gloria Steinem. We were secretaries and nurses and teachers, but only until, as our mothers prompted us, we found "Mr. Right."

Remember?

Yup, I thought. *But that river of reveries is slowly ebbing and drying up.* So my inner child gave me some advice: "Look," she said, one eye on her smart phone, the other on her lollipop, "This stuff is hysterical. You've got to write it down. Chronicle it. Make sure those kids who don't know what a Polaroid camera or a rotary phone is get to read about when their aunts, or grannies, or that strange cat lady down the block, were young. Give them a slice of what life was like when women wore miniskirts and teased their hair until it gave up, and guys wore leisure suits and enough jewelry to make the queen jealous. "And you better do it fast," she nagged, "...before you forget."

So that's what I did. I wrote down my experiences in the past lane and solicited help from some pretty funny ladies, writers who've been there and done that, who graciously offered to share stories about their first kiss, their fixation with disco dancing, their tanning machine fiascos, the stigma of wearing patent-leather shoes, and the fact that they once believed in flower power, making love not war, and being suspicious of anyone over thirty.

Still, my pesky inner child insisted that, while I was at it, I should fast forward to "now" and include some funny-side-up stories about what it's like to go from hot pants to hormones, from bell bottoms to Birkenstocks, from mood rings to menopause. So that's what I did. And this time, more funny ladies came forth to share episodes like an ex-husband's cremation ceremony, a "You-don't-look-anything-like-you-do-on-the-singles'-site" dating experience, the art of surviving a millennium office, the battle of the bulge, and more.

All of this is in the book you're about to read. We wrote *Laugh Out Loud* so we'd have a record of when we were young and when we were old. Both time slots were certainly ripe with material. We, like, think this book is rad, totally far out, and groovy. And, readers, we hope you do, too.

And get this. Not only will this anthology take you back and forth in time, an added bonus is you could lose weight in the bargain. See, experts tell us 15 minutes of laughter a day will burn 10 to 40 calories. That's enough to shift about one to four pounds a year. So for anyone looking for a fitness routine that doesn't involve movement of any body parts, or cutting down on essentials like New York Cherry Cheesecake with a grande moca cappuccino crème frappe, this book's for you. Grab a chair, put your feet up, and exercise yourself silly.

Just LOL.

—AZN

"We dance for laughter, we dance for tears,
we dance for madness, we dance for fears, we
dance for hopes, we dance for screams, we are
the dancers, we create the dreams."

—ALBERT EINSTEIN

I Came to Dance
by Michelle Poston Combs

You know how people say they wish they had been born in a different era? Like they wish they had been a flapper, or grew up in the age of The Big Bopper and sock hops?

Not me.

I was born in early 1963 at precisely the right time. I was just the perfect age to experience the '80s dance clubs. And, boy, did I love dance clubs. That's where big-haired women and sockless men gathered. That crowd fit me like a glove.

Every week was the same. I couldn't wait for the weekend—for the lights and the smells and the music. Especially, the music. I would count the days until Friday, and when it finally came, it seemed to pass at warp speed.

Being young and on my own, my budget only allowed for cover charges, but that wasn't a show-stopper. Guys often bought me drinks. And when they didn't? Water was free. Besides, I didn't go to drink. Like Stephanie, John Travolta's girl in *Saturday Night Fever*, I came to dance.

Before I knew it, though, the club was closing. One look at me and you could tell—I had a great time. When the harsh lights were brought up, my hair was stuck to my neck from layers of sweat and Aqua Net. My pink and blue eyeshadow was smudged, and perspiration had smeared my mascara and eyeliner so I looked like Alice Cooper might have, if he had sex with a raccoon.

Club night and date night were mutually exclusive. Clubs were for hanging with friends, not significant others. Negotiations on which clubs to hit were always fierce. The Glass Menagerie or The Crystal Parrot? Porky's or Caddy's? Or perhaps we'd go slumming and try the Tri-City Yacht Club. My friends always argued over which club was the coolest and which one had the hottest guys. Those things never mattered to me. Which place had the best dance floor? Which location played the best music? Now that was a valid debate. I came to dance.

In 1985, I lived paycheck to paycheck. I ate a

lot of boxed mac and cheese and ramen noodles. I wore cheap shoes (I valued quantity over quality.) And I owned stilettos in every color. My favorite shoes, though, were part of my best outfit. Acid wash pumps, acid wash jeans and jacket, with an acid wash vest underneath. (This was, obviously, my "acid wash" period.)

The best club was Porky's. I would walk in wearing my acid wash and I felt like a celebrity rocker, like Lita Ford, Sheena Easton, or Joan Jett. My friends were "minglers." So we usually parted ways early. As for me, I'd stake out a table near the dance floor, and wait until it was time. I was drooling to dance. But there was "walking waiting" involved. Being the first girl on the dance floor was lame. I've never been super cool. But I had no desire to be completely uncool, either.

Well, unless the DJ played "I Melt With You." I'm pretty sure all clubs had a requirement that you must dance when that song came on.

Now, honestly, I don't really miss those days. But I do feel nostalgic when I hear Billy Idol's rendition of "Mony Mony," or anything by Michael Jackson. And I am really grateful I was able to experience the '80s dance clubs.

These days, I still dance like no one is watching. But that's because no one is watching. I'm not quite as aggressive in my moves, and my footwear has changed dramatically. I retired my stilettos over 25 years ago. They only come out on the rarest occasion. For the past ten years, no occasion has been rare enough. So I sport sensible shoes.

Like I said, though, I still dance. I don't sweat as much as I used to and my venue is the kitchen. But at least it doesn't smell like booze, salt, and desperation. My husband's in charge of the music. As long as he throws in a few songs from my long ago, I'm happy. And when I hear an old club song, I'm transformed. I blink and turn into that same dancing queen I was all those years ago.

That happened just the other day. When I heard the opening bars of "Dancing with Myself," I dropped the potato I was peeling and jumped into action. A loud *POP, POP, POP* sounded through the music. My husband looked up from his book.

"Was that your knees?" he asked.

"It could have been," I said, continuing my gyrations.

"Maybe you should dial it back, Flashdance," he said.

"No way," I shouted back. "I'm not slowing down—not now when I have my own built-in percussion."

"Okay," my husband replied. "But don't complain to me tonight when you can't walk."

He's right, you know, I thought. *It's almost dinnertime and those potatoes aren't going to peel themselves. Plus, my knees are starting to feel a little shaky.*

I realized then that I can't boogie for hours fueled by nothing but hormones and foo-foo drinks anymore. That's okay, because bourbon is better than a frozen strawberry daiquiri any day. Then, too, instead of making me spin around in a sweaty mess for hours, these days, my hormones just make me a sweaty mess.

I'll take what I can, though, and be grateful I can still bop and rock at all. Because whether I'm in a club, or my own kitchen, (and even if my knees do provide the percussion)—I'm there to dance.

The Hotbox Girl Caper
by Amy Mullis

"Excuse me?" my father said.

"I'm going to be a Hot Box Girl," I repeated.

Mom looked over at me. She had her hands on her hips. "That better mean you're going to be packing pizzas to go, young lady," she said.

Explaining my role in the college play *Guys and Dolls* to my parents didn't go well. I was to play one of the co-star's chorus line backups, coyly called "Hotbox Girls" after the night club where much of the musical action took place.

My dad wasn't crazy about my decision. His idea of the perfect part for me would have been the second nun from the left in *The Sound of Music*. But I figured if I could parlay a little song and dance and a lot of stage makeup into fame, fortune, and extra credit in my drama class, maybe I could win him over after all.

But it wasn't easy. I needed more than a few lattes after rehearsals so I could stay awake for my late-night study dates. And then, because I was a commuter student, there was that long drive home. That's the time of the night nobody is on the road but other commuter college students and Officer Krumpkes.

If I were honest with myself—not a strong point when you're on your own for the first time—*Guys and Dolls* was not the best creative outlet for me. At 18, I was a case of snack cakes away from looking like a doll, unless you were talking Cabbage Patch. But, then, I didn't have to be gorgeous. All I had to do was sing a little and dress like a stripper.

Of course, I had no idea at the time that twenty years later, I'd wind up explaining my entertainment escapades to my teenagers.

"Thank God there wasn't any internet then," my kids said. "Imagine if my friends could see you in blue jean shorts."

"I know," I agreed. "Blue jean shorts are the pits."

I decided not to mention the stripper number, though. It was a clever song-and-dance extravaganza, and our dignity was preserved by pink polyester leotards. But even without the internet, the stigma of polyester lasts forever. In a game of "Fashion Failure Family Feud," polyester would surely be the number one answer.

Still, I remember that back then I felt quite fetching. I wore hot pants and a checked shirt tied at the waist for the "Bushel and a Peck" scene. I also wore so much makeup that I could have graduated from Clown College with honors. The barnyard scene seemed natural for me. I went to college. So surrounding myself with animals eating out of a trough was a logical second step.

I was wearing the hot pants outfit when the police stopped me.

It was a dark and stormy night, if you replace stormy with fog so thick you couldn't strain it through a chain link fence. I had no coat to cover my scanty costume, as I peered up at the spotlight and shiny badge. I couldn't help but rethink my decision to use the entire pod of Belize Blue eyeshadow. Stage presence was most likely not as important in a car late at night.

I told the nice officer that the fog was too heavy to see my hood ornament, much less the lines on the road. It sounded like a line from a play. The six tons of red lipstick that lined my front teeth as I bit my lip kept me from speaking plainly. My Liza Minnelli false eyelashes kept sticking together like seals doing a slow clap. And mist clung to the strands of my haystack hair, teased to six inches past perfection.

One look and the nice officer invited me to step out of the car.

Party Girl Olympic Games with the nice officer as judge ensued. I managed the "Fingertip-to-Nose-Touch" with ease and scored a perfect ten on the "Walk-the-Line" challenge. I could recite my name and address with clarity, except for a stutter of embarrassment. I even added a few bars of "Bushel and a Peck" to let him know I was serious about my stage career.

Next, the nice officer compared my face to my driver's license once more, shook his head, then opened his mouth and closed it several times. I'm pretty sure he wanted to ask for my autograph, but was too shy.

When he was satisfied that I wasn't a threat to myself or anyone else, he handed me a warning and told me I could go. Then he waited until I was safely on the road. He was still there when I looked in the mirror—probably trying to figure out what to put in his report.

The way I drove, I could have gotten home faster jogging with ski boots.

By the time I walked in the door, I was a mess. Nervous sweat melted my makeup into a mask that looked like a cross between a Mardi Gras puppet and the Phantom of the Opera. My eyelashes were flapping like a pigeon in a headwind, and the Aqua Net on my hair held in enough fog water to float a goldfish.

"I don't want to talk about it," I said to Mom. Then I slammed into the bathroom and started stripping paint off my face like an interior decorator refinishing a spare guest bath.

Half an hour later, I sat with my mother at the kitchen table nestling a cup of hot chocolate and feeling dejected.

"Now I know what you mean by 'keeping up appearances,'" I admitted.

"How so?" she said.

I slid the warning the nice policeman gave me across the table like an Atlantic City blackjack dealer.

"A bushel and a peck of makeup," I said trying not to laugh, "almost got me in a heap of trouble."

"Wearing a turtleneck is like getting strangled
by a really weak guy all day."

—MITCH HEDBERG

When We Were Fashionistas

by Denise Denton Thiery

Every generation has its share of weird clothing and hairstyles. And, inevitably, the generation before just doesn't "get" it. Still, when I look back, fashion might just have been as weird then as it seems to me now...and possibly weirder.

When I was in middle school in the early 1960s, our ensembles consisted of short-sleeved sweaters, poodle skirts or plaid straight skirts, and the ugliest shoe known to (wo)man: saddle oxfords. We wore bras so pointy and rigid, our boyfriends risked holes in their chests whenever we hugged them. And, under our skirts, we wore latex girdles as tight as tourniquets.

Though these medieval-like compressors gave our eyes a larger-than-life look, they made it difficult to breathe. So much so, that now and again, some of us actually fainted from lack of oxygen. It was an era of uptight restriction.

Back then, we "ratted" our hair until it resembled the Tower of Babel. Then we coated it with layers of hairspray until it had a hard, lacquered sheen that could probably have repelled bullets. You could have drilled three holes in it, and used it for a bowling ball.

Makeup was vapid. Our faces were dusted with chalky-white powder. Our lips coated with thick, nearly-white lipstick. Black eyeliner rimmed our eyes and extended out the sides, cat-like. We could pass for the love children of Vampira, the Goddess of Darkness.

Most of the boys, except for the "hoods," wore dress pants and shirts. They had their hair cut into "flat-tops," which I guess would have been handy if they had had after-school jobs requiring them to stand on their heads. The "hoods" wore their hair slicked back into something called a "ducktail." They dressed in tight, pegged pants and patent-leather pointy shoes, which tapped like castanets on the tile floors.

We girls were not permitted to wear patent-leathers. There was a theory these shoes could reflect the view under our skirts, and drive boys into a lust-crazed frenzy. Indeed, I always thought patent-leather shoes were undeservedly maligned, and that because of this bad rap, they languished somewhere in dusty warehouses, waiting to be sold to French Can-Can dancers or women of ill repute.

Purely in the interest of scientific research, one day I conducted my own experiment. I bought a pair of patent-leathers in a thrift shop, gave them a real Marine boot camp spit-and-polish shine, and took them outdoors to check the effect. The resulting glare temporarily blinded the pilot of a passing 747, who lilted to the left to get away from it. So there may have been some truth to the idea after all.

By the time I was in high school in the late 1960s, things had changed considerably. It was the era of liberation, and our fashions began to show it. Girls held elaborate bra-burning rituals in an effort to "turn those 'puppies' free!" And beehive hairdos, elaborate makeup, and restrictive clothing gave way to a more comfortable, natural look.

Makeup was light or nonexistent. Boys wore their hair mop-top style, thanks to the influence of the Beatles. We girls wore ours very long, stick-straight and parted down the middle. Those not blessed with naturally straight hair ironed the curls out.

Problem is, if you weren't careful, you could accidently give yourself a small, oval burn on your neck. Some people, my mother included, were quick to label the mark a love bite, or "hickey," which led to a stern lecture on morality, summed up as "No man will buy the cow if he's getting the milk for free." I didn't know what a lactating cow had to do with straightening my hair. But I knew there was a message hidden in those words. I just didn't get it.

Somewhere along the line, we decided that it would be "groovy" to dress like our great-grandmothers. We wore long, limp granny gowns with tiny floral prints, gathered just under the bust and trimmed with eyelet lace. We completed the look with love beads or a peace symbol on a chain. We wore wire-rimmed eyeglasses with tiny lenses, which we perched halfway down our noses. This gave very myopic girls like me peripheral vision as wide as a pair of drinking straws.

An alternative dress-up look was a micro-miniskirt in a loud psychedelic print. We wore these with fishnet tights, and white vinyl go-go boots or platform shoes with wooden soles three inches thick. These clunky shoes were so loud that during class changes, it sounded as if John Wayne and his posse were galloping into Dodge City.

The miniskirts prompted the invention of the one-size-fits-most panty hose.

The waistbands on these always seemed to cling precariously to my ample hips, while the crotch hovered somewhere just north of my knees like a mama kangaroo's pouch. Other girls had problems, too. Occasionally, as one of them was walking down the hall, this waistband would suddenly roll down, picking up momentum until it reached her ankles where it trapped and tripped her. Once in a while she'd be joined on the floor by one of her peers who had plummeted off her platform shoes.

For casual wear, both sexes favored faded plaid flannel shirts, untucked, and bell-bottomed, hip-hugging jeans—the wider, the better. The widest were called "elephant bells," and were so huge they could have sheltered a big-top circus. Fashion dictated these jeans cover our shoes and sweep along the floor, picking up dust balls, until the bottoms were tattered and filthy. This probably enabled the school to lay off at least two janitors.

So, now that I've looked through some old school yearbooks, I have this to say to any of today's teens I've made fun of for their fashion choices: Sorry, guys.

"I really don't think I need buns of steel.
I'd be happier with buns of cinnamon."

—ELLEN DeGENERES

Princess with a Lot to Lose Learns a Lesson

by Allia Zobel Nolan

Once upon a time, there was a beautiful princess whose initials were "A.Z.N." (It's my story; so never you mind.) When she came to be five-and-a-half decades old, a miscreant ancestor cast an evil spell upon her so that whatever she ate immediately settled as huge clumps of fat on her legs, waist, arms, and bum. Soon, none of her beautiful gowns fit. Worse still, she became known as "Her Porkness" behind her back.

"Hark, I must do something about this," she told herself one day. "Or I will become the laughingstock of the court." So the beautiful princess tried a liquid diet. She drank three chalice-fulls with each meal. It didn't work. She switched to an "Eat-All-the-Kumquats-You-Want-and-Lose" plan but got stomach cramps and had to quit. She also tried supping on nothing but mutton; then nothing but fish.

Finally, one day she noticed her corset fit less snugly. She had finally lost some weight. The spell must be broken, she figured. Ecstatic, she rushed to the kitchen for mead and sweetcakes to celebrate. The next day, her corset would not hook, and the beautiful princess hung her head and cried.

To cheer her up, the princess's cousin, Lady Bunns, of Steele, came to visit for a fortnight. After breakfast one morning, she suggested the princess join her for a chat as she walked around the court. The princess wasn't keen on walking. But she figured anything was better than sitting around watching herself get bigger. So off they went.

Bear in mind the princess's usual day consisted of eating, sitting, napping, eating, writing poetry, spinning yarn, some crewel work, and listening to the court minstrels. In other words, she spent a lot of time in her quarters on her keister. So getting out of the castle proved exhilarating—especially since it was summer, the air was fresh, and flowers were in bloom.

"I hate to admit it," the princess said to Lady Bunns, "but I'm actually enjoying this." The princess didn't quite understand what was going on, only that she had felt better and had forgotten about her problem.

"I take these jaunts often," announced Lady Bunns. "Thou art welcome to join me."

So the two started walking regularly. And as they did, they spoke of many things. Her Porkness—I mean, the beautiful princess—poured out her heart to her cousin, who in turn, confided that she, too, had been plagued with a similar spell.

"How can that be?" cried the princess. "You eat like an ox, yet art slim as a jousting lance. Tell me, Lady Bunns," she pleaded, "that I might do the same. How did you break the spell?"

Lady Bunns leaned in closer. "Well," she said, "thou must eat moderately."

"Oh, but I already do," wailed the princess. "In fact, there are times I practically starve myself."

"But there's something else," said Lady Bunns. "And you must do it not just for a month or six, or a year, or two, but ever after."

"Tell me. Tell me," the princess cried out even louder.

"Well, if thee must know, it's called 'exercise.'"

"Exercise!" the princess blurted. "I'd rather be boiled in oil."

Still, when Lady Bunns returned to Steele, the beautiful princess decided she had no other alternative than to do the dreaded exercise. She walked around the court twice a day and joined a spa in the next village.

Slowly, the fat melted off her, and six months later, she had lost 30 pounds. The same folks who had given her the porcine label now chided her "Thou art too thin," to which the princess retorted: "Eat thy hearts out."

When two years had passed and the princess was able to maintain her Guinevere-like physique, she knew the spell had truly lifted. In fact, she noted, as long as she pumped iron and took her daily constitution at least three times a week, she could eat most anything—even splurge on mead and sweetcakes now and again.

Sadly, Lady Bunns, of Steele, did not follow her own instructions. These days she is somewhere in Idaho modeling "big mama" gowns for women of substance.

The End.

"You can learn many things from children.
How much patience you have, for instance."

—FRANKLIN P. ADAMS

CLAP, CLAP, CLAP
by Tracy Roberts Buckner

I spent an afternoon with a few girlfriends. One of them asked me to help her load pictures from her camera onto her computer. I asked, "Don't you have three kids at home who can upload, download, boomerang, hashtag, video, and share anything faster than you can say the word 'Help?'"

"They have no patience for me," she responded.

Another girlfriend lamented, "My kids want to show me how to do something once and only once. After that, they put me off, roll their eyes, say they're too busy."

Seriously, I thought? *No patience? Too busy?*

I wonder how our kids would have fared if we moms had had the same impatience when it was time for potty training? Can you imagine us rolling our eyes when our kids needed their diaper changed, saying: "Really? Again?"

Or, when it was time to teach them to ride a bike without training wheels, how about if we said, "Didn't I just show you this yesterday?"

I'm sure most moms fondly remember being readily available to teach their kids how to throw a baseball, football, frisbee, to ice skate, swing a racquet, a golf club, do a cartwheel, ride a scooter. Just imagine their faces if we had said, "Are you kidding me? Does it have to be done right now?"

The list goes on and on of what we did with patience and smiles during those "mothering years." Those were the years my kids didn't know or care that their mother used to work for an impressive, large corporation, with her own office, her name stenciled on the door, and her own secretary. I was clearly on the career path to somewhere important—back when I wore heels and gave a crap about how I looked from the side.

Many of my friends and I got off that path willingly and instead spent weeks, if not months, patiently explaining to our little ones how to tie one's shoelaces, sip from a cup, brush those little teeth. And then, when these milestones were finally accomplished, we'd clap like they had won a Pulitzer. We moms made those kids feel like they were kings and queens of their world. You put your own socks on?! *Clap, Clap, Clap!* You pulled your pajama pants up?! *Clap, Clap, Clap*! I clapped so much I had calluses.

I can't remember ever once rolling my eyes at my kids. Can you?

I didn't think so.

A friend of mine had the best retort when her son complained about being asked to help her with her iPad. "Look, do you know how many months it took me to teach you to use the toilet? So, sit yourself down and explain this to me. I wasn't born connected to the internet," she said.

Right on, girlfriend.

Yes, technology issues need to be explained a few times before I'm proficient. But does anyone need to be reminded how many times we had to show our kids how to hold a fork ? How many math flash cards we held up? How many vocabulary lists we listened to being recited over and over again?

I get the feeling our kids think if they just ignore us we'll figure out techie things on our own. Maybe we should have tried ignoring them when they needed us to teach them how to grab a Cheerio.

Recently, I decided to make an old-fashioned photo album from pictures saved to my phone, Facebook, Instagram, and my computer. Like most of my friends of a similar age, I had hundreds of pictures spread over many devices and apps. But what good were they? Did I ever ask anyone if he wanted to see pictures of our summer vacation, a 60th anniversary party, a graduation, and then, just hand over a disk? Not likely.

So, I channeled that confident corporate gal I used to be, conducted my research, and did a few trials and (many) error uploads to my computer. I didn't ask for any help; didn't need anyone's patience; didn't want to disrupt any oh-so-busy schedules. I did it on my own, thank you very much.

First, I learned to Photoshop, so that nobody looked better than me. I also eliminated the red-eye effect, cropped photos, made backgrounds lighter or darker, added text, and designed an album cover. I gathered and uploaded from many apps and across many devices...no small task for someone my age.

Then, happy with the final product, I electronically ordered a hard-copy album and shared the online version with my friends and those oh-so-brilliant, uber-busy, hyper-connected, impatient, kids of mine. And get this, for the online version, I ADDED MUSIC!

I felt like raising my arms and playing the theme song to "Rocky."

As I hit "send," I secretly wanted someone to clap, to say "Yay!," to give me a prize, a ribbon, a trophy, any form of congratulations—like I had done for my kids for so many years.

So, of course, I called my mother.

And, being the super mom that she is, she clapped.

"I hate it when I'm dining with older people and
the waitress asks me if I want a kid's menu."

—KAYLA LAYAOEN

Kathy
May we always
have lemons
Kelly

Lemon Aid
by Kelly L. McKenzie

For as long as I can remember, I've always
looked younger than I actually am. I haven't
always been happy about that.

Take, for instance my 10th grade school
dance.

For once in my life, I wanted to look my age,
not my shoe size. I wanted to stand out, or at least
blend in, with the other girls. But to do that, I
needed the help of my sister, Wendy, who was 18
and savvy. And, with much whining on my part,
she finally caved in and agreed to be my beauty,
fashion, and dance consultant.

Wendy's advice was right on target. First off,
one had to wear the right fragrance. Citrus was in.
So, the plan was that minutes before entering the

gym, I'd drench myself with lemon. Not the juice of the actual fruit. Something even better: "Love's Fresh Lemon Cologne," purported to be "the power of a zillion lemons in one little spray," according to the advertisers. As an older, more experienced girl, Wendy confirmed it: no boy could resist a walking lemon.

Whether it was because—or in spite of—my fruity aura, Wendy insisted I wear lemon seersucker bell-bottoms that matched perfectly with an embroidered Mexican peasant blouse. To complete the ensemble, she picked out yellow leather platforms that added a good three inches to my five-foot-two-inch frame. I was aging by the minute.

My sister also performed wonders on my long, normally flyaway, mousy-brown hair. She parted it in the middle and flattened it out with gobs of Dippety-Do Setting Gel. I made a mental note not to go near any open flames.

"I look like a sick Cher wannabe," I cried when I eyed myself in the mirror. But Wendy insisted the style was more like the unfortunate Jenny from *Love Story*.

"You remember," she said, "the girl who was terminally ill and died."

I took her word for it.

As for my makeup, I was secretly grateful that we had already had several prior run-throughs because the blueberry eyeshadow Wendy troweled on from my eyelashes to my eyebrows had taken quite some getting used to. Still, surely the heavy eyelids added to my older mystic.

So, after a mere two hours of careful preparation, I finally looked my age, not the usual five years younger. I was thrilled.

But one thing still worried me.

As the 10th grade class president, it was my job to book the band. Someone had given me the number of a local agent and when I called him, he immediately told me about "Mother's Sweet Little Secret." As incentive, he played a 30-second taped demo. I wasn't sold. My tastes ran more to the soft pop tunes of Michael Jackson, Neil Diamond, and The Hollies. He brushed aside my concerns.

"Look," he said, "You're lucky they're available. This'll probably be their last school gig. You won't get a chance like this ever again. They'll be too expensive."

Geez. I thought. *Our school could miss out on an opportunity like this, simply because of me?* I had to say "Yes."

As the day of the dance approached, Reverend Mother cautioned everyone to allow enough room "for the Holy Spirit" between us and our dance partners. She needn't have worried on my account.

I never learned how to slow dance. Instead, my sister concentrated on teaching me "the Funky

Chicken," rationalizing that no boy could fail to be impressed by a girl dressed in yellow, flapping her wings. In the end it didn't matter.

The boys asked the same girls they always asked to dance—the girls who didn't need gobs of makeup or wacky hairdos to look sophisticated. Meantime, the rest of us lined the gym walls, painfully enduring four hours of loud, thumping music, with several extended guitar solos. Not surprisingly, that was the last I heard of Mother's Sweet Little Secret. Hopefully, they changed their name and moved to another country.

My own mother had a bit of advice for me when I slouched in for breakfast the next morning.

"Honey," she said, "Let me tell *you* a little secret. You might not like looking younger now. But you sure will when you're older."

It wasn't until 1983 that I finally got some hope the tide had turned. It was on a trip from Sydney to Alice Springs in Australia. I was 27. The seat belt sign had been off for only a few minutes when the willowy blonde stewardess delivered a heart-stopping message.

"The pilot is wondering if you'd like to visit him in the cockpit," she informed me.

Like to? I'd be thrilled! As I floated behind her up the aisle, my thoughts raced ahead unchecked. *Whatever would the pilot and I talk about? Would we go out afterwards for drinks?*

As I stepped into the cockpit, I noticed there were at least six other people there as well. The pilot grinned at me and clapped his hands together.

"Welcome everyone! Now that you're all here," he said excitedly, "I'd like you to look out the windows at the fluffy clouds below. Who can tell me their scientific name?"

As everyone shouted out a variety of answers, the penny finally dropped. My companions were all enthusiastic children. The pilot thought I was one of them.

Now, that was a tough one. It took me several years to get over it. But, yes, Mom was right. Somewhere around the seasoned age of 50 or 55, I did begin to be happy that people mistook me for younger.

Thankfully these days, my looks have somewhat caught up to my age. And, in my view, everything is as it should be. I'm delighted to look and be 61.

Still, on those odd occasions when I do have a hankering to feel decades younger, I simply reach for a lemon. One whiff, and *poof!* I'm back in 1972, dousing myself with cologne. I'm sweet sixteen again, wishing I were older.

"The brain is the most outstanding organ.
It works 24 hours a day, 365 days a year,
from birth until you fall in love."

—SOPHIE MONROE, *AFFLICTED*

My Love Affair with Robert Redford

by Carolyn Anderson Jones

In 1967, I was eighteen, naïve, full of life, and trying to decide whether I should go to college or join the Peace Corps. I believed in flower power, making love not war, and I didn't trust anyone over thirty. That year the hit movie, *Barefoot in the Park* was released starring Robert Redford and Jane Fonda. I was smitten with the movie, but more so with its male star, Robert Redford.

Barefoot in the Park was a delightful comedy/romance about newlyweds, Paul and Corie, who were desperately in love, but also desperately mismatched. Paul was a serious, young attorney eager to make his way in the world. Corie was a free spirit, eager to experience everything life had to offer. I wanted to be Corie. I wanted to move to New York City. I wanted to marry Robert Redford. Running barefoot through any parks was optional.

I really bought into the "Barefoot" life. I was idealistic back then, and had dreams about finding my soul mate and living happily ever after. Everything was going to be perfect. He and I would walk in the moonlight, chase butterflies, pluck mountain flowers, make fanciful bouquets, and fall asleep in each other's arms every night. We'd have perfect children, meaningful careers, and if we did have arguments, they would always end with magical make-up sex, just like in the movies. (Cue the hearts, flowers, smiley faces, puppy dogs, and violin music.)

Yeah, like, that's what really happened. The reality of it all was I did get married, and like the average mother in the 1970s, instead of chasing butterflies, I chased kids. I spent most of the best years of my life changing diapers, cleaning carpets, doing mounds of laundry. I went to work exhausted, smelling of eau de baby—not Chanel No. 5—and wore clothes stained with baby spit and burped-up formula.

What's more, instead of walking barefoot in the park, I walked through a minefield of Legos and half-eaten crackers. And don't even get me started on romantic dinners, date nights, or any of that walking in the moonlight stuff. Totally nonexistent. And sex was a fleeting memory as we fell into bed, worn out and drained, and were asleep in a heartbeat. (Cue the dogs barking, kids crying, frowny faces, and cats screeching in the backyard.)

Fast forward fifty years. Robert Redford and Jane Fonda recently starred in a new movie, *Our Souls at Night*. It's a tender story about two lonely, widowed adults, Addie and Louis, trying to make a connection. The two seniors don't know each other, but forge a friendship when Addie asks Louis to spend the night with her—totally platonic, no strings attached, no ulterior motives. She just wants someone to share a bed with and talk to. That's all.

Well, sorry, I am not buying into this premise, thank you very much. I'm kissing up to the age of 70, much older and wiser now. And I know for a fact that I wouldn't want a strange man spending the night in my bed, and here's why:

Nighttime is ugly when you're old. It can be ugly when you're young, but more so when you've reached the status of "elderly." That's because old people snore, break wind, groan, sputter, and drool all night. And since I'm guilty of all this as well, I'd rather not have some stranger watching and listening.

Plus, on a good night, I get up once to go to the bathroom. On a bad night, maybe three or four times. On an even worse night, I'm back and forth like a yoyo. And if I had a man in bed with me who had the same problem, well, I'd never get any sleep. And he wouldn't either. I'd be very grouchy in the morning. He probably would be, too. Just saying.

Then, there's "bed head." You know, when it looks like your hair had a party in a wind tunnel and you can't get a comb through it? I look my absolute best when I first wake up. NOT! I can barely face myself in the morning mirror, much less submit some strange man to the scary sight.

Finally, there's "morning breath." Blech! That's all I need to say about that.

So, as far as I'm concerned, the movie producers should have reversed the story line. What I'd have loved to have seen was Addie knocking on Louis's door to ask if he'd spend the day with her, instead of the night. Days are better. No bad breath or bed head. You're at your best— showered, presentable, and raring to go.

Later on in the movie, Addie and Louis eventually did share days with each other. And it was beautiful. They went fishing in the mountains, had lunch in town, and enjoyed trips to fun places. To me, that was far better. Days equal beautiful. Nights, not so much.

Still, I wouldn't say "no" if Robert Redford ever knocked on my door in real life and asked if I'd like to spend the night with him. Not a chance.

See, I'm in love with him. So much so that I'd be willing to deal with any snoring, passing wind, groaning, sputtering, and drooling, should a miracle happen and the movie star wind up in my house.

I'd just make sure I woke up before him, gargled with mouthwash, and ran an industrial-size comb through my bed head. (Cue the hearts, flowers, smiley faces, puppy dogs, and videos of lovers running barefoot in the park.)

Saturday Night 'Ain't' What It Used to Be

by Allia Zobel Nolan

I recently took a breather from Netflix and caught a rerun of *Saturday Night Live*. John Travolta, light years younger, in tight pants and gold chains, was strutting his stuff on the dance floor, and it brought back memories. As an old (or shall I say mature) married lady, Saturday is just another night for me. However, it wasn't always that way.

Saturday night used to be "date" night, an evening no respectable single woman ever stayed home alone. So if your plans didn't include dinner with a gorgeous hunk—or failing that—a beer with the guy you met at the Laundromat—you were obligated to at least hang out with your pals at the Marriott, where there was loud music, available males, and expensive daiquiris with as much rum in them as there was in a glass of Yoo-hoo.

This ritual was supposed to not only give you something to do, but could also land you a date for the following Saturday; and then, if things clicked, every Saturday night thereafter—except if you got married—and then you could both stay home.

I spent a lot of weekends socializing like this with my friend, Sheila. Truth is, though, I never really enjoyed it. I wasn't a fancy dancer. And try as I might I never saw anyone who remotely resembled the Adonises my friends all swore were always there. So, one weekend out of the blue, I decided to break the "Saturday night solo taboo." I told Sheila she should go on without me. I could probably have just as much fun at home.

In retrospect, not everyone would have given my evening four stars. And unfortunately, there were some setbacks. There was zip on TV— sitcoms and films like *Planet of the Apes*. And by the time I checked the video store (this was pre-Netflix and HBO, remember), all the clerk had left ranged from *Kung-Fu* movies to a tape on *How To Repair Your Toilet Tank*. I tried reading the flaps of *War and Peace*, but that gave me the munchies.

So I did a *Cosmo* quiz, ate a ham sandwich, then busied myself dialing Rigolini's for some take-out.

Martha Stewart wasn't around then. So I had no idea I could even attempt to do crafty-type things, like make filigree milk chocolate leaves from scratch, or stencil the inside of my refrigerator. But as I recall, I did finally wind up having a modicum of constructive fun. I gave myself, my three cats, and the toes on the tub a pedicure. I took off all the address labels on my stack of magazines. And I sifted a bunch of lumps out of four tins of flour.

My pizza arrived, and I remember the delivery guy tried to make a pass. When he asked why a "looker" like me was home Saturday night, I told him I had rabies. Then, because I was feeling a tad sorry for myself, I downed the whole pie, a liter of diet-cola, and a box of Oreos. I was so bloated when I got in my bubble bath, the water overflowed.

Next morning, Sheila called to fill me in on what a great time she had, and, of course, on the fabulous guys I missed. There was the Latin actor with the (alleged) Mercedes who presented her with a rose (which he most likely stole from the lobby bar flower arrangement). He would have danced every dance with her, she said, had his estranged (fourth) wife not gotten drunk and jabbed him in the eye with a piña colada stirrer.

Another beau I missed was the "to-die-for" muscleman student, who was working his way through an "Applied Mechanic's Helper" correspondence course. He was a super gentleman, Sheila said, who offered her buffalo wings from the free buffet. He took her number as well as the five Absoluts she bought him because he left his wallet in his other pants' pocket.

Another real cutie, Sheila explained, was the suave, sandy-haired, blue-eyed mortician. His family owned a string of funeral parlors—and he promised to take Sheila on a tour, show her the latest in embalming methods, and give her some makeup tips.

Looking back, I still say it was a toss-up as to who had the most fun. So, now while I sit with my hubby binge-watching *Mad Men* and munching on diet, low-sodium, low-fat popcorn, I can truly say Saturday night sure "ain't" what it used to be.

And, sugar, that's just fine with me.

"I do yoga because punching people
is frowned upon."

—ANONYMOUS

Twist and Shout: My Life In and Out of Yoga

by Karla Araujo

I admit it. I'm a yoga backslider. My adventures in this ancient Indian pursuit began about forty-eight years ago. At the impressionable age of twelve, I borrowed a book from the library featuring a cover photograph of a dark-complexioned man, his limbs rubbery and coiled into a peculiar pose. I was hooked.

Making the leap from Nancy Drew's *The Secret in the Old Attic* to Swami Vishnu Devananda's *The Complete Illustrated Book of Yoga* might seem quantum to some. But I was ripe for conversion.

By then, I had graduated from the Monkees'

"I'm a Believer" to the Beatles' "Sexy Sadie." It was 1968 and the Fab Four had embraced the Zen master Maharishi Mahesh Yogi's teachings, joining him in his ashram in the foothills of the Himalayas. *If sitting cross-legged on the floor was cool enough for the Beatles,* I thought, *it was definitely cool enough for me, a churlish suburban Washington, D.C. preteen.*

But after a week or two of holing up in my bedroom impersonating a pretzel, I realized there were other, more entertaining forms of adolescent summer fun I might be missing. Top of the list was hanging out at the pool with my friends, eavesdropping as the older girls discussed—in encyclopedic detail—what went on at night in the back seat of the Pontiac Firebirds and Ford Mustangs parked along the neatly manicured streets of our neighborhood.

Cobra pose, alone in my bedroom? Or, my friend Teri Sue's latest installment of Sex Ed 101 imparted on the dank benches of our swim club's locker room? No contest. *The Complete Illustrated Book of Yoga* was returned to its dusty shelf in a quiet corner of the library. At least, for that summer, my spiritual enlightenment would have to wait.

Over the next four decades, in my perpetual search for holistic health, I tried everything: Dancersize, body sculpting, Jane Fonda videos ("Hot cross buns!" still echoing in my fitness flashback), step aerobics, running, tennis, weight training, power walking, and Nia movement classes. But by the time I was fifty, work deadlines, divorce, tumultuous romances, geographic relocations, and the sudden death of my mother added up to a gargantuan wake-up call. I may have been fit, but I was stressed, exhausted, and anything but tranquil. I needed a better way.

In the spring of 2006, I was living on Martha's Vineyard. Yoga was booming on the island, with devotees lining studio floors from wall to wall. In fact, yoga was booming everywhere, with an estimated sixteen million Americans practicing on a regular basis. Anusara, Bikram, Kripalu, Kundalini, Vinyasa, local venues offered a cornucopia of options with unpronounceable names. I decided I'd take another crack at it.

I entered my first yoga class with trepidation. After all, it had been four decades since my last attempt at lotus position. But one look at the instructor convinced me I was in the right place. She was tall and lean, with long shapely legs, high firm breasts, a flat stomach, and regal posture. She moved—rather, glided—across the studio. And her face was the picture of serenity. Yoga had obviously transformed this woman into a peaceful, willowy beauty. I had high hopes it would do the same for me.

"Does anyone have any physical issues I should be aware of?" she asked. *Should I mention my meniscus surgery, chronic lower back pain, and torn rotator cuff?* I thought. When none of the other eighteen participants spoke up, I decided that suffering in silence must be a key virtue of yogis and yoginis.

While daily, my lower back, neck, and wrists cried out in pain, I became addicted to the equanimity (described in the brochure as a mental calmness, composure, and evenness of temper, especially in a difficult situation), I achieved with each class. I was definitely less stressed. I could even navigate across Martha's Vineyard at the height of August traffic without mowing over oblivious cyclists, moped riders, and pedestrians, making do with an occasional, "Jackass!" or "Moron!" hollered out my window.

But my father's failing health brought me back to Washington, D.C., after twenty-five years of moving around the U.S. Dealing with his crises, there was no time for yoga, and my fitness regimen disintegrated into an occasional walk or tennis game sandwiched between visits with doctors and tours of assisted-living facilities.

Along the way, I acquired a new partner, Randy, a retired attorney-turned-abstract painter who embodied the kind of natural quietude I could only dream of. As I made my way around the frenetic nation's Capitol in my tank-like SUV, I reverted to pre-yoga behavior, shaking my fist and flashing the bird at drivers while my Buddha-like boyfriend urged me to go to my "Zen place."

"#&@% you, you idiot!" I screamed out my open window as a cocky twenty-something in a new Camaro tailgated me. "Stay in your own lane, loser!" I warned a woman whose cell phone texting rendered her unable to pilot her VW with any degree of accuracy.

Perhaps it was time to return to yoga. My waistline had thickened. My thighs were chafing. My mood was sour. My sleep fitful. I'd entered the phase doctors refer to as "perimenopause" (Latin for "the beginning of hell"), characterized by the ebbing of estrogen and its accompanying murderous rages. Could yoga serve as a substitute for Prozac, Xanax, Hormone Replacement Therapy? It helped me once. I would try again.

I found my way back to the yoga studio a couple of months ago. Call me an optimist, but after only a dozen classes, I feel more serene. And so far, my body is uncomplaining. While I did nearly come to fisticuffs with a very unreasonable woman in the parking lot recently, I managed to score a prized spot without police intervention.

And although Randy did suggest, midway through that altercation, that I go to my Zen place, with the help of my renewed yoga program, I feel like I'm nearly there.

"Take care of yourself now that you're old enough
to know how. Drink water, sleep eight hours
(I wish), and don't go within 400 feet of a tanning
booth or I'll slap you. Hard."

—OLIVIA WILDE

The Redder, the Better
by Lucia Paul

I had the good fortune to attend middle school in the mid-1970s. We didn't have cell phones, Instagram, or Facebook. Heck, we didn't even have beepers. We had landline phones, copies of *Seventeen* for the latest beauty tips, and the annual high school yearbook to check out how photogenic we were. Bad decisions were not immortalized forever, except in our memories.

Our mothers smoked and drank while pregnant. And none of us carried around a water bottle to make sure we were always hydrated. We also paid no attention to sun protection. I mean none. My daughter, who is now in her mid-twenties, was religious about sunscreen when she was in middle school. That could be because her generation knew more about the damaging effects of the sun. Or it could be due to my cautionary tale: "The Time Mom Went into the Tanning Booth with Her Best Friend and Lived to Tell about It."

My childhood best friend and I are still close, although she lives many hours away by plane. We don't talk for months. But, as women of a certain age know, when a BFF like this calls, you can pick up right where you left off without missing a beat. She's one of the smartest and most accomplished women I know, highly educated and respected in her demanding professional life.

Still, back in the day, she had the judgment of an inchworm. And I must admit, so did I.

Even before the "redder is better" tanning incident, the two of us engaged in a lot of shenanigans. A Greatest Hits of our naughty behavior includes: highlighting our brown hair with Clairol Frost and Tip. The end result of this effort was orange tiger-striped strands, which we proceeded to cut out with scissors; wearing matching space helmets and walking our ten-year-old selves into a singles' bar to see what would happen; and laughing so hard in church that the minister, who was my friend's father, asked us to leave. The list goes on. But the tanning booth incident remains the most shining example that the adolescent brain is not fully formed.

For the sake of this story, I'll call my friend "Marge." Her mother belonged to a health club and we often tagged along. We'd swim in the pool, go in the sauna, buy Cokes out of the vending machine, and basically hang out. Remember, this was long before kids could while away an afternoon taking duck-faced selfies, though believe me, we would have done so non-stop if we'd have had the chance.

The ladies' locker room at the club had a (believe it or not) free, unattended tanning bed. You could just walk into it, set the timer, and begin the glorious frying process.

It was the last Sunday of spring break and school started the next morning. Marge and I had both been away with our families. So we had some color. But we decided that we weren't tan enough. We wanted to be golden brown. Coppertone tan— not the slightly red color we both were then. We'd be the envy of everyone at school. With that, a genius plot was hatched: We'd take turns going into the tanning bed, come out, and decide if we were golden brown enough. If we weren't, we'd simply go back in and bake some more.

I know. It's hard to even read phrases like "free and unattended tanning bed," "golden brown," and "bake some more." In case you're naïve in the ways of the tanning bed, let me assure you that even today, there is no "emerging golden brown." Even though it's still ill-advised to tan in a booth, bed, or even in nature, it is always a process that's done slowly, over time.

But back to 1975. We set the timer and began. We started with, maybe, eight minutes, came out and decided, "Nope. Not tan enough yet," and back we went. Luckily, after maybe only two rounds, one of us observed, "My face feels kind of hot. Does yours?" To which the (now lobster-colored) friend replied, "Yeah. Maybe we should stop."

In the time it took Marge's mother to finish her Ladies' Aqua Aerobics, we both knew this had been a terrible idea. So we started crying. When her mother saw us, we fessed up to what we'd done. Even though she was a minster's wife, she must have been a pretty good poker player because she was as calm as could be, despite the fact that she drove me home with lightning speed.

We got to my house and Marge's mom explained to my furious parents why we looked the way we did. It was mutually agreed that Marge and I should have a cooling-off period (literally), given the fact that every time we were together, something dire and drastic happened—mostly to our appearance. We both went to the doctor the next day, and so weren't the envy of anyone. We missed our big first day of school. The good news was that both pediatricians determined that if we had not had the "base tan" of our recent vacations, we'd have been in much worse shape.

These days, Marge and I both have daughters who are the same age. They have never met. When they were younger, my BFF and I agreed that with their lineage, this was probably a good idea.

Still, we hope they do meet someday, now that they're both adults. And we'll have sunscreen ready, just in case.

> "All the good music has already been written
> by people with wigs and stuff."
>
> — FRANK ZAPPA

to Kathy —

Everything Old Is New Again

by Lori B. Duff

Lori B. Duff

Everything old is new again, they say, and just as you can actually find leg warmers for sale, and actual fashionable teenagers who wear them, other '80s things are making a comeback as well.

Vinyl, for example. After we agreed that earrings were a no-go for my son's birthday, he decided he wanted an old-school turntable. Not that he owned any records himself. But he had heard that music sounds better on records and that some artists are now releasing albums on vinyl. He wanted to be among the first to get them.

So, I bought him a turntable. And a super-duper one at that. It had USB ports and auxiliary doodads he could hook up to his iPhone or computer or whatever, and, theoretically, he could even copy the tracks somehow, which I thought might also prove very useful. I gave the turntable to him the morning of his birthday. He was really excited, despite the fact that he had nothing to put on it.

"Mom, don't you have some old records in the basement?" he asked. And with this request, I went on an archeological expedition in the vast strata of detritus in my cellar to find my old collection. I finally unearthed it, grabbed a handful—including some 45s—and brought them upstairs.

Now, my son is a teenager, five foot, nine inches with a very low voice. He looks very manly. So I forget there are some things I consider basic that he hasn't a clue about.

Looking back to when my children were babies and I was new to this whole mothering thing, I was shocked to find out how much children didn't know. That was one of my favorite parts of parenting, watching these little fleshy lumps become fully formed people who could, with instruction, drink from a straw, use a spoon, and find their own toes on command.

I remember one incident in particular. When my son, Jacob, was six weeks old, he caught a cold. He wasn't terribly sick, as far as illness goes, but his little body wasn't equipped to handle a

stuffy nose. He had no idea that he could breathe through his mouth. And he didn't have the motor control to sniff or blow his nose.

So he'd breathe through his nose, find himself unable to do so, panic, and then cry, which made him breathe through his mouth. He'd realize that he was breathing again, settle down, then close his mouth, and the cycle would repeat. I'm the kind of mean parent who thought this was hilarious and videotaped it.

Eventually, I took pity and used the booger-sucker thing as best I could. And somehow, he lived another fourteen-plus years.

That's what I thought of when I handed Jacob my vintage Duran Duran "Rio" record and he looked at it, and then the turntable, and had no idea how to put the two of them together to make music.

I told him to put the hole in the record on the pokey thing, which he did fairly easily. But he didn't know what to do next. So I found myself explaining the concept of the spiral and the needle and how the whole trick was to not make that *skrrrrritch* sound because that would mean you are scratching the record. I added that I've managed to go since 1982 without scraping "Hungry Like the Wolf" and that I might be justified in killing him if he did it now.

Next, I explained how we got our music in

the old days: We used to go all the way to the record store to buy 45s. There was no downloading singles instantly from iTunes when a song came out. I told Jacob not to judge me by my collection of 45s, which included Phil Collins' "Against All Odds" and "Let's Hear It For The Boy" by Deniece Williams, but by the fact that I actually had one of those plastic thingamabobs you need to fit a 45 on the spindle still wedged firmly in a record.

He also found out that playing a 33 record at 45-speed and vice-versa is good for a few laughs.

I learned a few things from Jacob's introduction to the way we were, too: "Footloose" still makes me want to dance. My dancing is a different kind of embarrassing than it was in 1984. And, when I hear an oldie but goodie, I don't care who sees me, I'll dance anyway—even under threat of a video posting. (You can't shame me. I'm a mom.)

And turns out? My son actually liked some of my records. I smile when I hear him listening to them when I am not in the room.

We did know how to have fun back then, and music is still music and can still move us together, even if we are decades apart.

"When people show you who they are,
believe them the first time."

—MAYA ANGELOU

When It Comes to Men, Honey, Nothing Is Better Than Nothing

by Allia Zobel Nolan

"Better than nothing" may be okay when it comes to a job. It may be okay when it comes to money. But when it comes to relationships, I have serious doubts.

In my opinion, no matter how old you are, or how lonely you think you are, it's better to cut your losses than to stay entangled because any relationship is better than none.

I didn't learn this overnight. Like other women (when I was single), I kissed my share of frogs hoping they'd turn into princes, and when they didn't, pretended they had just the same.

Ultimately, I came to my senses with enough warts to teach me that, though the story of the white knight might be a fairy tale, there were nice men out there—but I wouldn't find them if I was spending all my time sipping wine with Quasimodos.

There are women, young and old, who'd disagree. I hear them complaining all the time. On talk shows, in the grocery store, at the hairdresser. They recite a litany of horrible things their men do—gamble, cheat, wear polyester. But then, they defend them with adages such as "Nobody's perfect," "Beggars can't be choosers," "A good man's hard to find," "At my age, I have to take what I get," and my favorite, "He's better than nothing."

Sad part is some women really believe that. They'd make excuses for the cannibalistic serial killer, Hannibal Lecter, if they thought he was prime for a relationship.

"So what if he has strange tastes in foods," they'd say, taking his part. "Not everybody's a meat-and-potatoes guy. Besides, he has nice eyes and he's great with my dogs."

The possibility of having a relationship, any relationship, makes some women (who generally have 20/20 vision) suddenly myopic. They refuse to see even the most glaring flaws, putting up with guys even men wouldn't share an umbrella with if it were raining bullets. They know there's plenty wrong, but kid themselves into being optimistic. They view the glass as half full even when there's no water in it at all.

I remember a friend of a friend who felt this way. She went out with a guy for years who was a skinflint when it came to presents, only to discover he had an account at Victoria's Secret and bought lingerie by the shopping bags full. As if that weren't bad enough, it wasn't for other women, but for himself. She cried and moaned at first when she found out. But when I asked if she was going to stop seeing the dolt, she became indignant.

"What for? We get along great. And it was just a phase. He went to a therapist and he's fine, now. He hasn't bought a slip in three months."

Hello? Is anybody home?

What about these women who marry criminals, or guys on death row.

Surely, they don't think they can reform them? Or do they? That reminds me of another incident.

A woman I know met this guy at a bar, then started dating him. He was a bit quiet and laid-back, but she said she could tell he was nice because he was so tender with her cat. When I met him, all I could think of was the Pillsbury Doughboy. He was as pale as a ghost. Turns out he'd spent "some" time "inside." Robbery and various other things, she told me later with a straight face.

"But they were only misdemeanors," she said. "And he was probably framed."

Am I the only one who thinks stuff like this is strange?

Another woman I know spent eight years with a guy and it was obvious the "relationship" was going nowhere. She was a lovely person and deserved better. "He's not ready for a commitment yet," she said to me one day. "I don't want to be pushy."

Women are all too quick to blame themselves when things go wrong...especially as they age. They think, *Maybe I was too hard on him. I'm no oil painting myself, so I can't be too choosy. Maybe I'm the one who has the problem. Maybe I'm way too old, too fat, too tall, or a bore.*

Ladies, don't sell yourselves short. In all my years, I've never heard a man say he was dating someone he wasn't crazy about because she was "better than nothing."

Why? Because men think more of themselves. I think women should, too.

Confessions of My Younger Self

by Janene Dutt

A few weeks ago my computer was about to go into hard drive failure. With the threat of losing all my photos, videos, and files from the past 17 years looming large, I went into panic mode.

I frantically scanned through my Word and Excel documents looking for those that were imperative to copy, when the title of one jumped out at me: "Hannahsvomitingschedule.xls."

HANNAH'S VOMITING SCHEDULE: (PARTIAL LISTING)
DATE TIME TYPE COMMENTS

Date	Time	Type/Comments
11/27	9:00 PM	Projectile Vomited, no other symptoms of illness
10/29	8:00 PM	Projectile Vomited, runny nose, cold
11/24	6:00 PM	Regular Vomited after crying hard
11/25	9:00 AM	Regular Vomited in high chair
11/30	8:00 PM	Regular Vomited after drinking 8 oz milk, fast
12/15	2:00 PM	Regular Vomited after getting head stuck in luggage at store
12/17	6:00 PM	Regular Vomited after eating dinner at Cocos
1/19	1:00 PM	Regular Vomited immediately after eating lunch at IHOP
1/26	9:00 PM	Projectile Vomited immediately after drinking bottle of milk
2/10	12:00 PM	Regular Vomited while sitting in stroller
2/17	8:00 PM	Regular Vomited after choking on bread
2/21	8:30 PM	Both Vomited immediately after drinking bedtime bottle
2/28	10:00 PM	Regular Woke up from sleep and vomited

Upon opening the spreadsheet (and marveling that I wrote it), I was immediately transported back to my days as a young, first-time mom—the days I documented absolutely everything—food, sleep, weight, words. You name it; I had a spreadsheet for it. Now, to be fair, the kid clearly had a puking problem. So I was probably playing the good mom, trying to figure out a pattern or something. But, man, the level of detail here. I mean, just how could I possibly differentiate between projectile vomit and "regular" vomit?

As I sat pondering this, memories of my parenting style with our first baby came flooding back. Things like:

- refusing to let anything non-organic pass through her lips
- playing a "Brainy Baby" CD incessantly to ensure her developing synapses were properly stimulated
- scrubbing down grocery carts with anti-bacterial wipes and then placing her in a cushy cart cover that made it impossible for her to touch the cart anyway
- driving past dozens of local pediatric offices to nearly the next county so that she could see famed pediatrician Dr. William Sears. (Hey, the guy wrote, like, 30 parenting books. Doesn't that make him way more qualified to chart her height and weight?)
- reading the aforementioned parenting books diligently
- fleeing the playground when I saw a kid with a runny nose as the child's mother attempted to explain that her kid's not sick: "It's just 'allergies.'" (Sorry, lady, if it's green, I'm gone.)

Fast forward 18 years and two additional kids later, and while I'm admittedly still a bit of a germaphobe, suffice it to say, my parenting style is a bit more "chill." (That's code for I'm a lot older and really tired.)

For example, when my second child, Jack, was about seven years old, he ran into a parked car in front of our house. He was hysterical, with blood gushing from his eyebrow. As a new mom, I would have completely freaked out. But I was now a more experienced, more relaxed mom of two. Yes, I was proud of how calm I remained as I cleaned the wound, stuck a dressing on it, and sent him back outside to play. Not so proud later on that night when it turned out that the kid actually needed 12 stitches, not a Spiderman band-aid. Oops.

A conversation the other day between myself and my third child, age seven, proves I'm not the mother I used to be:

Ava: "Can I have another cookie?"

Me: "You've already had two. No."

Ava: "If I eat one grape, can I have a cookie?"

Me: "Speaking of grapes, when was the last time you even had a fruit or vegetable? Seriously, you eat too much junk. Go eat five grapes."

Ava: "Then can I have a cookie?"

Me: "No!" Pause. "Ok, eat eight grapes and you can have a cookie."

Ava: "I hate grapes. Forget it."

Mind you, this was nine in the morning. Looking back, I'm sure my younger self would have been appalled that I even tried to bargain with my child.

Now, with this third child of mine, I sort of relaxed my parenting guard. She did not have to read ten books a day, has never seen a flashcard, has taken more than one nap in a dog bed, and, as a toddler, rode underneath the filthy grocery cart because, hey, why not?

Still, I think, as a result of me not doing everything, my youngest child can do anything. When she wasn't even two years old, I accidentally got locked out of our house while she was still inside. She couldn't reach the lock to open the door and soon realized she was on her own. I watched from the window in amazement as she waddled over to the pantry, poured herself some cereal in a cup, and sat there happily munching away. Clearly, she had learned to be self-sufficient because I stopped being so efficient.

Getting back to the vomiting chart, I kept thinking about it for days. I didn't know why, but I couldn't get it off my mind. Then the light bulb went on: What became clear, in that ridiculous spreadsheet, was how much control and knowledge I had over this child's life. It was so easy back then to be aware of every single thing she ate, every place she had been, every time she was sick.

These days, my little girl's all grown up.

She's 18, and has just left for college. And I would give anything to only have to worry about her not getting germs from the shopping cart again.

Instead, all I can do is breathe a sigh of relief when she texts me late at night that she's safely back in her dorm, try my best to chill, and hope she's eating enough veggies.

"There are no bad pictures; that's just
how your face looks sometimes."

—ABRAHAM LINCOLN

You. Are. Awesome!
♡ Jill

Camera Ready
by Joanne Salemink

I went shopping with my teenage daughter last
week. It was exhausting.

Not the walking, or the browsing, or the credit
card swiping, but the posing, the primping, and
the selfie posting. Time was when a person had to
be a celebrity to get that kind of 24-7 photographic
coverage. I realized, then, and not for the first
time, how glad I am to have come of age before cell
phones and their johnny-on-the-spot cameras.

At the risk of sounding like an old
curmudgeon (yes, that sounds like something
an old curmudgeon would say), photography has
changed since I was young. Back then, we used
to walk ten miles...in the snow...uphill...and down
again...just to drop off our film at the drugstore for

developing. (My apologies to any millennials who may be reading this and confused by the words "film," "developing," and "drugstore." Oh, yes, and "walk," too. These are technical terms we older folk used back in the day.)

Let's start with how the equipment has changed. While I'm not daguerreotype-old, I do harbor vague recollections of something called a "Polaroid Land Camera Automatic." It was a big, impressive looking camera, with a telescoping lens on a folding bellows (which I was told repeatedly not to play with), and it used "integral print film" that developed right before your very eyes.

That's right, whippersnappers. You aren't the first to use a camera that gives you a photo instantaneously. Of course, in my day, you had to stand around flapping a damp, smelly print until it dried enough to peel back the protective cover and watch the image finish congealing. Or not. We were always a bit hazy on how this miracle worked, how long the developing process actually took, and whether you flapped and then peeled, or peeled and then flapped.

The Land Camera was relegated to the back of the closet when we traded it for a lightweight, small and modern—but still boxy—Kodak Instamatic. I lobbied my parents for the even more modern, smaller, flat, pocket Instamatic 110. And, no sooner had I done this, then that futuristic design was also eclipsed by the super-skinny Disc camera. I swear, I was the last girl in my 4-H club to get a Disc camera, much to my chagrin. In fact, soon after we bought a Disc camera, point-and-shoot 35 millimeter cameras became the way to take pictures. Who knew?

So I was exposed to four different cameras, four different types of film cartridges, two different flash cubes (built-in flashes became *de rigueur*), none of which was interchangeable.

Then came the digital. No more film, no more developing, no more waiting. No more wondering: Did someone have their eyes closed? Was my finger covering the lens? Did I center the picture? Or did I cut someone's head off? No longer did we have to wait—sometimes weeks—for the answer to those and other burning questions. We thought one-hour (one hour!) printing was a miracle. With the advent of digital cameras, though, we could view our shots right away. And, then, choose whether or not to print them.

That's right, kiddos, when we were growing up, we were kind of in the dark about our pictures. In fact, we had to get an entire roll of film, 12, 24, or 36 shots, developed, and prints (sometimes two sets) made of each picture, without knowing if the photo was a dud or not, whether the picture was worth it.

Not only that, but we paid for everything—

bought the film and flash cubes, footed the bill for developing, then paid to have prints made. So, the economics of photography were drilled into us at a young age. We didn't just waste film, willy-nilly, taking pictures of whatever caught our fancy. No siree, Bob!

Today, most images never see the shiny side of photo paper. Instead, they bounce around in the cloud, passing from screen to screen to screen, destined to remain digital. Forever. That's fine for some. Yet, I miss holding a physical print in my hands. I miss sitting shoulder to shoulder with friends and family, pointing and laughing as we pass around piles of prints. I miss trying to pocket the photos I feel make me look anything less than Miss Universe.

Of course, it would be non-curmudgeonly of me to ignore the poor judgment some youngsters nowadays show by posting glassy-eyed party pictures to the Insta-snap-twit-chat site-of-the-moment. I recognize that "inebri-happy" look from pictures (ahem) I used to take of my own friends. (Oh, and the "duck-lips, kissy face pose?" You kids didn't invent that, either.) The difference is that my pictures, fading and curling at the edges, are stashed in a tote in my basement, while yours are floating around the internet for the entire world to oogle.

I know (tsk, eye roll, hair flip) you think those

photos can only be seen by your "friends" and only for a millisecond (another tsk, eye roll, hair flip for emphasis). And maybe that's true. I hope that's true. I'm willing to believe that's true, because I'm more concerned about what you're missing out on by constantly being tethered to a camera. There is life outside your cell.

But despite my inability to take a decent selfie, I'm not a Luddite. I recognize the convenience of having a camera always at hand—especially during an all-too-rare reunion with friends. When the conversation finally slows, we sigh and wish that one of us had thought to bring a camera, that is before we all realize we all brought cameras, because we all have cell phones. Duh.

Maybe that's the difference between my middle-age mindset and that of my daughter's generation. For the most part, I save my picture-taking for—something worthy of my taking a picture—not, say, because my eyebrows are "on fleek." (Google it.)

Because, let's face it, if I waited for that to happen, I would never take another picture. So maybe things haven't changed.

"As for himself, when he went to go to a party,
as one was sometimes obliged to, from a wish not to
give offence, he walked into the middle of the room,
said 'Ha! Ha!' as loud as ever he could, considered he
had done his duty, and went home."

—VIRGINIA WOOLF

It's Party Time
by Sherry Stanfa-Stanley

Lots of little things suggest we're not as young as we used to be: Spying ourselves in some clearly distorted mirror. Concluding that sleeping until noon is way more a waste of a day off than a constitutional right. And enduring that first colonoscopy or skin cancer exam. (Really, you need to check there, too?)

Yet the signs aren't obvious in only how we look or what we do. They are also apparent in what we say—or more accurately—what we don't say.

For example, it seems I rarely find occasion these days to use the words "mosh pit." (For those who're drawing a blank, "moshing" is a type of dancing that has people slamming into each other at a concert in an area known as the "pit.") Oh, how I love that term, and I still dig a great concert. Yet, surprisingly, no one dove into a mosh pit the last time I attended a James Taylor show.

Also, I have never, not once, uttered the words "fo sho." Until last week.

Stymied while trying to conjure up words that people my age don't use, I queried my twentyish son. After he sent a few suggestions, I wrote back, "Thx. These are perfect. Fo sho." Because that's the kind of hip and aware parent I am. He texted back, "Really, mother? Sigh. God help us all."

But most noticeably of all, the word "party" has practically disappeared from my vocabulary.

At one time—roughly age 14 to 24—"party" was a mainstay of my vernacular. It showed up liberally in everyday conversation, particularly in the form of a high school hallway plaintive plea: "Is anyone having a party this weekend?"

And "party" was an equal opportunity word. We were also fond of using it as a verb, as in, "Hey, we have an algebra quiz next period. Want to go out to the parking lot and party instead?"

We employed various derivatives, too, the most popular being the noun describing a person, such as, "Yeah, dude, he's a really cool teacher. I heard he's a partier."

Oh, man, the parties where we partiers partied in our youth. For me, they included my ex-boyfriend's bash that the police crashed and then the local news station came to cover with its new, breaking-edge "mini-cam." And the one my two older sisters hosted—when the front door was destroyed and the repair fund collected from helpful partygoers was stolen by a couple of uninvited guests just before my parents arrived home. They were party poopers, for sure.

I was mostly an innocent bystander at those. But later, when reading in our high school newspaper, just before graduation, that I was voted Best Party Giver, my perplexed mother asked, "When did you have parties?"

Figuring I was practically college-aged and had little to lose anymore, I shrugged and replied with a near-smirk, "Every night that you and dad went out."

(Disclaimer: This was the SEVENTIES, people. Have you ever watched *That Seventies Show?* Even many of the nerdy kids partied around the table in their basement, while their parents were right upstairs, watching TV. I was thoughtful enough to wait for mine to leave, which practically made me a teenaged saint.)

But those crazy youthful years are just a memory. A foggy one, at that. And few people my age have parties anymore.

These days, we "have people over" or we have a "get-together." When we do use the term "party," it's always as a noun, and it describes a fully different event than those of our teens and twenties. Now, it's a dinner party or a silver anniversary party or perhaps a gender-reveal party for our new grandchild.

Unlike our high school or college years, it no longer seems quite appropriate to host a party by supplying a couple of bags of Doritos and asking everyone to pitch in for a keg.

We plan an elaborate menu, being certain to cater to every taste and diet. After all, this is the new millennium. Someone is sure to require vegan, low-carb, or gluten-free.

Looking back, the most popular parties I hosted after my late twenties included a piñata, a case of juice boxes, and a bunch of five-year-old rugrats. Wild? Yes, but nothing in which the local news stations or police seemed to take an interest. Although I could have used a couple of officers to handle crowd control.

We seldom party in the same active verb tense anymore. Many of us haven't touched anything in the under-the-counter drug category in years. Oh sure, we may still imbibe in more than mild amounts of alcohol from time to time. (When I say "we," I mean "you" not "me," of course.) But we don't usually say we partied too much. In my crowd, we prefer to use more sophisticated terminology, vaguely suggestive of being victims of circumstance. We say we were "over-served."

We're still a fun bunch, those of us who are post-thirty (or post-forty or fifty). Most of us enjoy a good get-together, a few laughs, maybe even a few drinks. We play a crazy game of charades, talk about the good old days, and sip a glass or two of Pinot, while we pretend to be wine connoisseurs.

But we no longer break down doors, sit around a basement table in a fog, or draw nightly news coverage.

Sure, we may not say the P-word much. But darn it, we still know how to have a good time. And I'll bet, if we dudes and dudettes gave it our best midlife effort, my generation could still rock and roll all night—and party every day.

That is "fo sho."

Letters from My Past

by Karen G. Anderson

When my 70-something parents sold their place in Massachusetts to move to a condo, they needed to dispose of my memorabilia. Over the years, it had moved from desk to file cabinet to boxes in their basement. So, they gave me a choice: the boxes could go to the town dump, or they could be shipped to me in Seattle.

That's why, on a damp January evening, five battered boxes thumped onto my bungalow porch, one of them splitting open from age and impact. I dragged the mess inside and shoved everything into a cupboard. It wasn't until the following summer, in need of closet space, that I confronted the task of sorting through the stuff.

It was worse than I'd feared. I opened the first

box and a profusion of Richard Brautigan novels and psychedelic concert posters spilled out—along with a few packets of rolling papers.

Toss. Toss. Toss.

The last box I got to was stuffed with old letters. The rubber bands keeping them in bundles had disintegrated with age and they had fallen into odd juxtapositions. High school gossip, penned in curlicue script with pink felt-tip markers on day-glow green stationery, lay beside angry poems from college friends, scrawled on paper torn from notebooks and folded tightly in ways that radiated anxiety.

Nearer the surface of the heap drifted letters from old boyfriends, interspersing stories about the women they'd left me to pursue, with their vague hints that our relationship still had...possibilities. And there were tissue-thin pages from women who, as I recalled, had always snubbed me to my face.

"Dear Karen," they all had the audacity to begin.

Why had I kept these letters from college and beyond? More to the point, why had I ever opened them in the first place?

And now, here they were, back to remind me that I've had a lifelong inability to discard useless things, from bad-boy lovers to past-its-date cottage cheese. This box of old letters was piled high with the incriminating evidence.

Clearly it had to be destroyed. Armed with a

shot glass of whisky—I brought the bottle along in case things got really bad—I sat down and started to sort through the papers.

Out went the letters from my high school crush, Andy. He was a nice suburban kid locked in eternal psychological combat with his dad, a Vietnam-era Air Force general straight out of *Dr. Strangelove*. In his cramped, spidery script, Andy penned self-pity and vitriol.

He complained about his family and about the southwestern "Moo U." where an unfortunate combination of astronomical SAT scores and abysmal grades had landed him. He cursed rednecks, frat boys, and New Agers alike. Andy fled into the Arizona desert. His last letter whined that his then-girlfriend had driven off with his pickup truck, abandoning him at a roadside gas station. *How picturesque*, I thought, as I tossed his missives aside.

And out went the letters from Sue, now a quasi-famous New York designer. (I'd seen her profiled in an avant-garde magazine, swathed in a fashionably ghastly black outfit, her pale face frozen in an expression of terminal boredom.) Sue's high school letters read more like diary entries—the kind that are intended for later, autobiographical use.

"Up at 4. communed with the lake, the willows," she gushed, her typing free of encumbrances like capital letters or periods. "would visit, but feel I must spend these last, precious weeks *en famille.*"

I shook my head. This was when she was preparing to leave for college in Maryland—all of 50 miles away.

The letters weren't all so ridiculous. My friend, Miriam, now an anthropologist and mom in Pennsylvania, had sent postcards and letters as she hitchhiked and biked through the Rockies, Alaska, Europe, Mexico, Central America, and the Deep South.

She'd chronicled the 1970s and 1980s the way I remembered them, from drug busts ("I asked myself, she wrote, 'Miriam, what are you doing with these weirdoes?'") to Earth Day activists and bicycle freaks ("This guy in a Mercedes tried to run me off the road," the letter read. "So, at the next light, I snapped off his antenna.") to fears of approaching Yuppiehood ("I'm standing in the kitchen," she scribbled, "it's all neat and clean and the kids are downstairs watching TV. Am I getting the Housewife Complex already?"). God, I miss Miriam.

I moved on to the letters from my 30s. Those went much faster: Wedding invitations from couples long divorced. And Christmas letters from people who, after my own divorce, had sided with my ex-husband and vanished into the same deep, dark abyss I uncharitably hoped that he was in.

I looked at the clock. It was getting late. In fact, it was nearly midnight when I stood up and surveyed the avalanche of dead letters at my feet. My first thought was to take them out to the recycling bin, but that seemed too kind. Perhaps it was time for the garbage?

Then inspiration struck. I scooped up the papers, rushed to the fireplace, stuffed them in, and lit a few matches.

I refilled my glass. Then I settled down on the couch with the marmalade cat and we watched as my past fricasseed. In less than ten minutes, ashes were all that remained of nasty Andy, pretentious Sue, and that insufferable biologist from New York...what was his name? Too late. It was gone forever.

Oh, there were a few more I should have tossed. Probably the letters from Peter, a college crush who'd haunted me through graduate school. Peter wrote concerti, had a radio show, sculpted with a blowtorch, and went to medical school while touring with his rock band. I was the first woman he'd ever slept with. After we made love, he beamed with delight and announced that he was going to buy a bottle of champagne...for his therapist.

I'll get around to his letters next time.

> "Even snakes are afraid of snakes."
> —STEVEN WRIGHT

The Snake Lady
by Leslie Bamford

"You should go and see Mimi on Bridge Street," my classmate told me, her pearl earrings dangling above the obligatory green tunic and school tie of our school.

"She'll have your ears pierced in no time," another girl chimed in. "We've all been to the Snake Lady, except you and Joanie. You're both too chicken."

I wondered what unusual features would make a woman look like a snake. But I didn't think on that for too long. Truth be told, I was afraid of having my ears pierced, by anyone, whatever she looked like. Still, I was determined not to be labeled a coward like my goody-two-shoes friend, Joanie. I was even more determined not to face life wearing those clip-on horrors that my mother wore—the ones that made painful dents in her ear lobes. Or the ones she tried to make me wear that screwed on, like a torture rack out of the Dark Ages.

Yes, I would do it. I would face my fear and be the first person in our family to ever have her ears pierced. I knew better than to ask my mother for permission. She had always been clear that girls in our family would never stoop to such a low-life practice.

So I went rogue, made an appointment with the Snake Lady, and headed downtown on the bus, my mother's voice in my head saying that nothing good ever happened on Bridge Street.

Mimi the Snake Lady's sign advertised ear-piercing, fortune-telling, and tarot card readings. I could feel my heart beating against my chest wall as I rang the bell, opened the door, and walked up the long, dark staircase to her apartment. I had always had an aversion to needles, or anything that was going to poke holes in me. This was no exception. I could hardly breathe.

Mimi opened the door. She was tall and thin, with a gold scarf wrapped around her head, blood-red lipstick, and gold hoop earrings dangling on each side of her neck. But she didn't look like a snake after all. The girls must have been pulling my leg.

I stepped inside. The lights were dim and as my eyes adjusted, I saw a room full of statues.

There were snakes on the windowsills, under the tables, on the shelves. Red cobras stood in strike position in corners. There were snakes everywhere.

Then I saw it—the real thing—a brown-striped rope beginning to uncoil on the beige carpet. Mimi saw me look from her face to the floor. She saw the horror in my eyes. Without a word, she nonchalantly stooped down and lovingly picked up the writhing reptile, turned, and put it into its case on a nearby table. Then she closed the lid. I exhaled a bit too loudly.

Mimi led me into another room. It was filled with dozens more snake statues. I didn't dare look too closely, in case one of them was moving. I just sat stiffly, willing myself not to bolt upright, as the Snake Lady pierced my ears. I barely felt the pain, my fear of snakes overwhelming any normal bodily reaction I might have otherwise had.

Afterwards, I paid and then stumbled back down the stairs, with metal posts stuck in my wounds and instructions on how to avoid infection floating around in my head. I looked over my shoulder once to make sure nothing was following me, and emerged back on the street, unscathed. The thought of facing mother's wrath went fleetingly through my mind. But after all those snakes, I figured I could handle anything.

Fifty years later, I look back and wish I had asked the Snake Lady to read my palm as well as pierce my ears. Perhaps she could have warned me about some things to come.

She could have told me not to marry my study hall friend from college during my "looking for Mr. Right" phase. She could have explained that when our divorce came through, I'd lose a husband and the brother I never had. She might also have advised me that the next guy would never have worked out, either, although he appealed during my "back to nature" phase. She could have alerted me that the first aid supplies in his log cabin were non-existent, and that I'd have to cure my one-and-only-earlobe infection one weekend with Tanqueray gin.

What's more, she might have foretold that I'd finally meet the love of my life much later, that my earring collection of chalcedony, turquoise, and moonstone would see me through any ups and downs, and that some things, like true love, really do last a lifetime.

But there could have been more live snakes in her apartment, so it never occurred to me to stay any longer than necessary. Instead, I went out into the world with holes in my ears, and found my snakes elsewhere.

My phone rings and breaks the reverie. It's Joanie from school, the only one who kept in touch all these years, calling long distance to chat. As always, the conversation turns to our youth.

"Did I ever tell you," she asks, "that my mother had a bottle of Valium in the medicine cabinet? I used to steal pills when I was stressed. They helped me mellow out."

I'm speechless. Joanie, the same Joanie who was too strait-laced (or was it chicken?) to get her ears pierced for *her entire life,* admitted stealing pharmaceuticals from her unsuspecting mother? And she didn't tell me? Sure, I took cigarettes from my father's packs of Du Maurier, but Valium? I just wished she had told me back then, so I could have insisted she share. A couple of those little blue pills would have made my trip to the Snake Lady way more tolerable.

I tell Joanie this and I can hear her crack up laughing.

"Mimi, the Snake Lady?" she says, "whatever made you think of her?"

"Oh, nothing really," I say. We chat for another while, and after more reminiscing, it's time for goodbyes.

I hang up and walk to my dresser, open a small box, and pull out a pair of dangling red cobra earrings.

I put them on, and stare at my reflection in the mirror. A smile slithers across my face.

"Here's to you, Snake Lady," I say, and turn out the light.

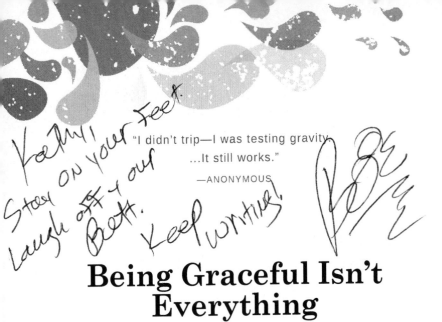

Kathy!
Stay on your feet.
Laugh off your
Butt.
Keep writing!

"I didn't trip—I was testing gravity.
...It still works."
—ANONYMOUS

Being Graceful Isn't Everything
by Bonnie Jean Feldkamp

Whether it's *Grease, Miss Congeniality,* or *Princess Diaries,* I love makeover movies. They take me back to a dorky, clumsy, adolescent me. A rebel and feminist, I recognize now that changing one's self for the admiration of the opposite sex was (and is) so wrong. But back then, I wasn't the most coordinated of kids. So I wanted a magical transformation to happen. Unfortunately, there weren't enough dance lessons in the world to grant me that grace.

In sixth grade, I traded my ballet slippers for band class. When the director suggested I try percussion, I exhaled in relief. I knew it was a good fit and that I'd have died playing something dainty like the flute. I also knew better than to try to march in the marching band. So in high school, I played pit percussion on the sidelines.

The band director liked to push us. We were a competition marching band, after all. We had a one-hour class during the school day, and he insisted we use it to practice on the field.

Now the steps to the band room led out to the football field. And the director figured we could haul our equipment outside, set up, and still have plenty of practice time before we finished and had to bring the equipment back inside. But each day he cut things closer and closer. We played outside until the class bell rang and everyone started to scramble. In that mad dash, as I lugged four timpani drums, a xylophone, and wind chimes, I often thought: *Maybe I should have taken up the flute.*

Still, I may have been a klutz, but I was strong. I could carry a timpani up the steps from the field to the band room all by myself. On one particularly rushed day, however, disaster struck. The wheel of a timpani caught the divider of the door and the rim of the drum crashed into my front teeth. I broke them both.

Two root canals and four hours later, I had new front teeth and no longer required braces. Plus, the gap in my front teeth had disappeared. This wasn't exactly the makeover I had hoped for. But it did end up being a quicker fix than my dentist had planned. What's more, the director filed his first band-related accident report. My fate was sealed.

Not surprisingly, my reputation as less-than-graceful didn't win over many guys. I mean, who wants to date a clumsy girl with fake teeth? A girl who lost her fingernail slamming her own hand in her locker door? Luckily, my best friend set me up on a blind date with a guy named Brad. He went to a different school and was unaware of my...um... problem.

On our first date, Brad and I watched a movie at his house. I figured this was a safe bet. I managed to maintain my composure while we made popcorn, poured sodas, and got to know each other. By the time I settled onto the couch for the show, I hadn't fumbled once. Brad even put his arm around me.

After the movie, I stood up to put the popcorn bowls on the counter. I knew my parents would be there to pick me up any minute. I said "thanks" and "goodnight" to Brad. Then I leaned over to give him a gentle kiss.

I hadn't noticed his loyal hound had wandered in and was sleeping at Brad's feet. I fell over the dog, punched Brad in the stomach, and proceeded to crash—face-first—into my horrified date's lips.

The dog whimpered. Brad bled.

"You bit me!" he yelled.

He was still dabbing his bloody lip with a tissue when I left.

I tried to put this faux pas behind me and focus on surviving the rest of the school year. I almost did, too. Then the basketball game happened.

The pep band pit, which was not actually a pit at all, was positioned above the visiting team's basket in a makeshift balcony. I played crash cymbals for the fight song. So I sat close to the railing, watching the activity below. We made an important three-point shot. And the director gave me the cue to begin.

The music was fast and I was to play a crash on every beat...that is until my sweaty grip on the cymbal strap slipped, catapulted over the railing, and landed in center court. Mid-play.

The cymbal crashed on the floor, then circled around and around, reverberating with each rotation. The referee blew the whistle, but the game had already stopped. Dumbfounded players, fans (everyone it seemed) stared up at the balcony. At me. I leaned over the edge and waited for the referee to hand my cymbal back. It was the only time in my high school's history that a timeout was called because of a band member.

I turned to my friends on the balcony.

Applause rang out. Tears stung my eyes as I sheepishly took a bow.

"Why do you guys even hang out with me?" I asked later. "I'm a walking disaster."

"Are you kidding?" One friend responded. "Life with you is full of surprises."

"Never a dull moment," another chimed in.

The rest were too busy laughing to say a word.

My clumsy display replayed in my head and I had to laugh, too. I guess it *was* pretty funny. *Maybe I am klutz*, I thought. *But I'm a klutz with a knack to make people laugh.*

I still am. And what would life be without a little laughter? For my good-humored friends who helped me then and continue to help me laugh at myself now, I'm grateful. For the rest of you who may be lucky enough to witness one of my spontaneous fumbles, "You're welcome."

'Take a Letter, Miss Jones'

by Allia Zobel Nolan

I f space were allotted by the number of different "hats" business people wore, secretaries (aka administrative assistants) wouldn't sit in cubicles. They'd have offices the size of a football field. Indeed, with the exception of mothers and housewives, few people do so many things, so fast and so well.

Still, stereotypes are hard to shake. And the old movie and TV portrait of the clock-watching, gum-snapping Girl Friday, (think *Nine to Five* and *Mad Men*), the girl in the tight sweater who made more phone calls than she answered is, unfortunately, a lingering one. Even in this day and age, admin assistants, like the late Rodney Dangerfield complained, are still notorious for "getting no respect."

Nevertheless, though the profession may not yet get all the recognition it deserves, it's a billion times better than when I sat behind a Selectric.

A typical secretary's day back then was full of clerical challenges. Mind you, this was way back in the BCs ("before computers"). Retyping mounds of correspondence—complete with yellow, blue, and pink carbon sets—was one of them. A stack of impeccable-looking letters would go into the boss's office—per his instructions—in the blue folder marked "For Your Perusal," only to bounce back out for another go-round covered in coffee stains, cigarette holes, spilled Scotch, red ink, and more arrows than the Indians used to fight Custer, in the green folder marked "Do Over."

At this point, the secretary would murmur a few words about the boss's birth mother, and start over again, using her innate problem-solving skills to figure out what went where, and her trusty handwriting analysis decoder book to decipher the worm squiggles that passed for the boss's penmanship.

This routine was interrupted about sixty times a day by a device the boss used to communicate, the signal from which (like one of Pavlov's dogs), the secretary was expected to respond to with certain predictable behaviors. One buzz—pick up the phone; two buzzes—come in for dictation; three buzzes—refill the jawbreaker bowl on the desk.

One long, continuous buzz was reserved for emergencies like the time the boss leaned back too far in his Exec-U-Chair, fell over upside down, and needed assistance to right himself. This code could also sometimes mean he was on an overseas call and his coffee was cold.

Secretaries were also required to "take notes," and a popular time for this was right before noon. Sessions usually lasted two hours or until the secretary's fingers froze in a crab-like position—whichever came first. While they dictated, at about 130 words-per-minute, bosses often ate lunch. So a secretary had to have a keen ear to catch what he was saying correctly, and a strong ability to concentrate should some airborne food fly out of the boss's mouth and go *splat* in the middle of her steno pad.

In those days, there were no "New Hire Welcome and Sensitivity Training Podcasts." Instead, an office manager, who got in a snit if anyone referred to her as anything but, showed secretaries the ropes and acted as mentors. Though all of the secretary's chores were on land, these Brunhilda-like individuals always gave instructions on how to keep a "tidy ship."

They also gave lessons on how to cater to the

boss's idiosyncrasies so as to avoid the fate of the previous 18 "girls" he had been forced to fire due to inefficiency or because they refused to be dinner escorts for important clients whenever said clients happened to drop into town.

These indoctrination sessions taught "the new girl" valuable tips on things such as paper clip placement, coffee bean procurement (brewing and serving), cigar ash containment and removal, not to mention gatekeeping (restraining associates and the boss's wife from bothering him while he taped his memoirs), banking services (ensuring that $5.00 a month was deposited in five different savings and loans for each of the boss's six children), and crisis management (finding a London Fog raincoat the boss could wrap himself in while the office manager sewed a rip in his trousers).

Okay, but that was the Neanderthal era, a time when secretaries relied on a different range of skill sets, chief among which was a heightened sense of humor. Today, (thanks in large part to technology and an increased corporate awareness of inanities on the job, power containment, and the outing of sexual harassment), secretaries are doing more of the work of a collaborative assistant (thus the name change), and less of the duties of an indentured servant.

Now if she can just get the boss to pick up his own shirts from the cleaners.

"'That's a lovely idea, Diana,' said Anne enthusiastically. 'Living so that you beautify your name, even if it wasn't beautiful to begin with...making it stand in people's thoughts for something so lovely and pleasant that they never think of it by itself.'"

—L.M. MONTGOMERY, *ANNE OF AVONLEA*

Jennifer Is the New Gertrude

by Jennifer Byrne

One of the first things I did when I arrived in this life was jump on the incredibly crowded bandwagon known as "Jennifer." Actually, it was my parents who heaved me on it, kicking and screaming. So I really had no choice.

"Hey, here's an idea," I imagine them brainstorming, "Let's give our new daughter the very same name as every other female infant born on Planet Earth this year. Sound like a plan?"

Blah! Being trendy is awesome—IF we're talking dogs, shoes, or purses, or dogs who travel with fashionable ladies who carry them in their purses. When it comes to a name, though, being part of the latest craze is the pits.

Your name, generally speaking, is supposed to be a unique personal identifier, a way to tell you apart from other people. When judged on that criteria, "Jennifer" is about as useful as being named "Hey, You." In my class alone at school, you couldn't drop a pencil without bumping into a Jennifer. There was "Jennifer M.," "Jennifer D.," "Jennifer B.," "Jennifer W.," and "Jennifer E.," otherwise known in schoolyard shorthand as pretty Jennifer, bucktoothed Jennifer, chunky Jennifer, picks-her-nose Jennifer, and Jennifer with the nerdy glasses (me).

Still, as time goes by, we will all morph into Old Jennifer, and even with extensive Botox and expensive face creams, we won't be able to hide it. Soon, before a person even meets us, she'll know what to expect: a geezette.

Here's why: when you have a name that's associated with a specific year, it's like a vintage of wine—it dates you. So instead of writing "Jennifer" on those little, square, white "Hello, My Name Is" conference tags, I might just as well write: "A '70s child," and let people guess. Chances are they'll come up with "Jennifer" without even thinking.

I'm told my parents named me after a character in the 1970 movie *Love Story*. (Spoiler alert: this woman dies tragically; thanks, Mom and Dad). Apparently, lots of other parents christened their offspring after this character as well, because Jennifer was the number one name that year—and for several years after. At some point, though, the name dropped off the charts and was squeezed out of the top one hundred.

The good news is I did manage to outlive my ill-fated namesake. The bad news is as we Jennifers move through the decades, our name has basically fixed us in time, and is pretty much tracking us across our life spans. It's as though we had been trapped by wildlife scientists, outfitted with Jennifer GPS collars and turned loose, with our names tattling on where we are at every step of the age continuum.

Once upon a time, being named "Jennifer" and especially "Jen" was a dead giveaway for being annoyingly young. For a while, "Jenn" with a double 'n' was favored as an even younger version of the name.

Today, we Jennifers aren't exactly ancient. But, we're certainly getting there. What I notice most about this is the terrifying way time has sped up. Years that once seemed to last—well, for years—now zip by at warp speed. I'm now the lady who tells embarrassed-for-me kids how they're "growing up too fast" and muses with old chums that our high school days "seemed like yesterday."

I've given this some thought, and the "over-the-hill" cliché explains it surprisingly well. I liken it to sledding: Trudging up the hill is like the first half of life. It feels like it's taking forever. But once we've finished the slog and start sledding down the hill, we're suddenly careening so fast we can barely breathe. That's like the second half. As my name now places me on the downhill slide, I'm hoping to put the brakes on and enjoy as much of the ride as I can before I hit bottom.

I can do just that if I keep in mind that gals who had trendy names like Bertha, Myrtle, and Gertrude back in the flapper days all too soon wound up trying to avoid indigestion, loose dentures, and telephone scams. So, if I'm ever going to enjoy myself, I'd better do it now.

I guess most of the '70s Jennifers are probably middle-aged like I am. Before we know it, though, we'll be bottlenecking rehab facilities at an alarming rate. Nurses will call out "Jennifer," and half the place will yell back, "Yes?"

This is my future. It's everyone's future, of course. But as a Jennifer, my telltale age will always precede me and rat me out. That is, unless the name comes full circle. Lots of things enjoy a revival. Everything old is new again. So I'm hoping that "Jennifer" will make a last-minute comeback. It could be the latest in recycled trendy names. Savvy moms across the country won't have to think twice. If they have a daughter, "Jennifer" will be their hands-down choice.

That way, maybe, just maybe, when people hear the name Jennifer and assume they're about to meet someone without a full set of teeth, they'd be right either way. They just won't know whether that someone will be an old lady...or an infant.

"I talk about wanting a boyfriend.
But I don't even know what I'd do with one.
Kiss him and then leave him in the corner?
How often does it eat?"

—WHISPER

For Kathy,
My wonderful fellow Mainer & friend
♡ Janine

First Kiss Misfire
by Janine V. Talbot

In 1974, Stephen King was in, Nixon was out, and girls were finally allowed to play Little League baseball. I was 14 that summer and looking forward to high school with its promise of romantic adventure.

Up to that point, nobody had taken my "Kiss me, I'm Italian" T-shirt seriously, and I might have run for the hills if they had. Still, by the end of summer, I was primed and ready. I was itching for my first kiss.

Before that, the closest encounter I had with the opposite sex was when my best friend and I exchanged stories about the Osmond Brothers (I had a crush on Donny; my friend worshipped Jay) and how we fully intended to marry them.

Having zero firsthand experience, we had no idea if our descriptions of intimate encounters with our potential future husbands were physically accurate. This was not a subject widely covered in *Tiger Beat* magazine. But we had fun daydreaming about it anyway.

Then, sometime in July, I was introduced to Ben—Benjy to his friends—through a teen youth group. He was a gangly 15-year-old with rust-colored hair and a million freckles. Benjy talked fast and had a sharp wit. And he towered over my five-foot-two-inch frame. Now this was usually a turnoff for me. But Benjy was an enigma who quoted Monty Python ("Spam, spam, spam, eggs and spam") and knew every song from *Jesus Christ, Superstar*. Best of all, he could sing. Back then, I was convinced I'd marry someone who would win my heart with his voice. So Benjy was looking better and better.

Our Saturday youth group activities typically consisted of bowling or roller skating, followed by a stop at our favorite pizza place. There was the occasional flirtation that will occur among teens in a social setting and a few obvious pairings off. But for the most part, we were a close-knit group of friends blowing off some G-rated steam.

We were driven between destinations and

used the time to belt tunes like "Seasons in the Sun" and "Billy, Don't Be a Hero" into the night air while the car radio blared through open windows. Benjy and I sat side by side and harmonized. And in those precious moments, I fantasized that one night he would stop in the middle of "Annie's Song," turn toward me, and tenderly place his lips on mine. I knew those lips had been around the block a few times, while my kissing was confined to practicing with a photo of Tony DeFranco from a glossy magazine cover. Still, I thought, *if I let Benjy teach me the ropes, I could be experiencing the real thing, and soon.*

One Saturday evening, before we went our separate ways, Benjy asked me if I'd take a walk with him. Summer was coming to a close and the night air had picked up a mild crispness, inviting us to inch a bit closer. I was giddy with anticipation. I discovered, though, that Benjy was no ordinary suitor. He had a whole shtick that was apparently part of his wooing technique. As we walked along, he began reciting a parody of "The Night before Christmas" that he said he had composed himself. This wasn't exactly what I had expected. I had hoped he would set the scene with something more like a Jim Croce song.

Now maybe on some other occasion, I might have been impressed. But this wasn't the time. Especially now that I had applied just the right amount of Bonne Belle Strawberry Lip-Smacker. I looked at him and couldn't believe how absorbed he was in himself. I thought about leaving Benjy alone with his stupid poem. But the night was beautiful and the stars shone around a waning crescent moon. It was the perfect setting. And I wasn't going to waste it. I was holding out for some romance.

Benjy put his arm around my shoulders as we walked, but the extreme height difference made for an awkward scenario. My hip kept bumping his leg, and his arm flopped clumsily on my shoulder instead of the strong, manly caress I had imagined in my first-kiss fantasies.

He guided me around the back of the building as he continued his recitation. That kept us from talking about anything else. Finally (and thankfully), he ran out of verses. Just then—as if on cue—a shooting star shot across the blue-black sky. Benjy knew a good segue when he saw it.

"Did you see that?" he said eagerly. "You're supposed to close your eyes, make a wish, and kiss the person you're with when you see a shooting star."

I was? Well, up until that point I had been fairly bored. So at least now things were starting to get interesting. I closed my eyes and pretended to make a wish. When I opened them, his face was within a few inches of mine. He leaned down. I leaned up, eyes closed again, lips appropriately puckered. Then it happened. Benjy planted a big, wet one—smack in the middle of my chin.

For a second my head remained tilted, but when I opened my eyes I was met with his embarrassed scowl. The moment hadn't just passed. It crashed and burned. I discretely wiped slobber off myself. Then, we walked in silence back to our friends. I don't even think we said goodbye.

On the way home, a sense of relief rushed over me. This wasn't supposed to happen with a boy I was just friends with. After the initial shock, I felt lucky he had such bad aim that night.

My first kiss would not happen for another year, with my first real boyfriend. It was an awkwardly perfect embrace between two sets of virginally parallel lips—just the right mix of comical and memorably mushy. That youthful romance wilted a few months later, but we did set off some fireworks for a short time. It just goes to show that you don't need a shooting star for the perfect first kiss. Sometimes the stars in your eyes can be enough.

"The only rule is don't be boring and dress cute.
Life is too short to blend in."

—PARIS HILTON

Look Good Trying
by Yvonne Ransel

I've never been the preppy type. This Italian face and my wild dark hair didn't seem to fit the monogrammed sweater look of the '70s. Even worse, those Peter Pan collars would always get in the way of my hoop earrings.

These days, I still struggle with the same Polo-image clothes in the golf shops I browse. Oh, the colors manage to change with the fashion world, lime green one year, periwinkle blue the next. But the baggy shirts and Bermuda shorts seem to be mainstays.

I've also never really been a crack athlete. So my mantra has always been "if you can't do something well, at least look good trying." I discovered this about thirty years ago when my children were active and I wanted a "sport" to get me off the bleachers and on to the playing field.

Tennis was big and free clinics were in abundance then. So I bought a Kmart racquet and hit the courts at one of our city parks. I rejoiced when the ball went over the net, but wasn't quite sure what to do when the smug instructor slammed it back at my feet. I wore jean shorts then, and a white T-shirt. It wasn't until I joined a proper racquet club that I realized the importance of a flippy little skirt and lacy panties.

Then there were the decisions: Do I choose Reebok, Adidas, or Nike? Was I finally becoming a jock? Who knew? Who cared? At least, I looked the part. I graduated to an oversized racquet costing close to $150 and had a drawer full of knife-pleated, box-pleated, floral, and plaid outfits.

I also knew tennis etiquette. After the matches, I'd strut my much younger body around the grocery store aisles and talk "game" with other players. I even entered a few tournaments. These turned me into a mad woman, with dark circles from sleepless nights and a turbulent stomach from the pressure. I did become stronger and more consistent, but never good. Still, I always managed to arrive courtside in the latest New Balance metallic.

Now skiing presented a larger problem for me: terror. At the slopes, I was bound in moon boots, snapped into bindings, and expected to propel my muffled body on an icy surface to "the lift," a contraption that slowed for no one. As it quickly rose above the trees (the trees!), I clutched the safety bar until my hands hurt, all the while gesturing to the lift handlers to get me off as soon as possible and without an embarrassing flop. Once on terra firma, I'd trudge to the top of a novice run, take a deep breath, and ignore the perspiration pooling in my armpits.

I could relax a bit then, and finally take in (what else?) the fashion statements. The colors on the snow bunnies and hot-doggers danced above the white snow. Hats, gloves, and neck warmers coordinated with their trim jackets and form-fitting pants. Did they look good, or what? Could they ski? Who cared? I, myself, truly tried for years to keep my skis parallel and to hockey stop. I never could, though. Speed would always force me into a dorky snowplow and I was grateful for the anonymity my goggles gave me.

On the other hand, I was made for après-ski. Who knew what run we finished on when we'd tromp into the Zoo Bar, thirsty for beer, our cheeks windburned, our hair matted? We could have been aspiring Olympians, especially when we shed our layers of expensive clothing. I remember one year, my outfit was pink and black; another year, green and navy. The last year I skied, fluorescent turquoise and fuchsia were the rage. That outfit still hangs in the downstairs closet.

Now that I've turned my attention to golf, I struggle with my drives, agonize over club choices, and curse every missed putt. At the same time, I rejoice in the walks among the pines and azaleas.

But, alas, dressing for these outings is still challenging. I know my legs would look better in shorter shorts, but Bermudas are the norm. And collarless V-necks would make my neck seem longer and slimmer. But nobody wears them. As for golf shoes, I'm definitely not a fan.

My mother is probably looking down from heaven, chuckling, when I lace up my saddle shoes before a round. How I despised those we had to wear with our school jumpers. Of course, saddle shoes are a little more colorful now, green or blue or burgundy. But they still do nothing for my calves. Ah well.

I have noticed recently that some younger women pro golfers have been sporting funkier outfits. So maybe there's hope. They probably realize how important it is to look good from behind—given all that bending and stooping and swinging.

As for me, I haven't found flattering golf shorts yet. But, this year, I did discover a real gem—a set of shocking pink golf clubs with a bag to match. I still don't know which club to use. But I have to say I sure look good searching for it.

A Single Summer
by Allia Zobel Nolan

Summers certainly are simpler now that I'm married. I can stay home and paint the porch. Or sit on the lawn, sip piña coladas, and watch my husband paint the porch. The point is I don't feel this immense pressure to have to *go* somewhere.

Most single women don't have that option. Come summertime, they are inexplicably driven by a mysterious gravitational force to join with others like themselves and take off to some exotic resort—(the kind advertised in scratch-and-sniff-the-air travel brochures)—ostensibly for some relaxation, but more likely to bag something that'll make the whole trip worth the money: a mate. I remember it all too well.

Cruises were the best buy because they stopped at more than one singles' hotbed, said our travel-agent-cum-Mary-Kay-saleslady one year when my friend and I were planning our annual getaway. Indeed, and if we had any savvy at all, she advised us, we'd choose what most of her unattached female clientele preferred: The Purple Paradise Fantasy cruise ship.

The Purple Paradise Fantasy cruise ship was a liner extraordinare, she swore, not one of those tacky, floating meat markets you saw on Geraldo exposés. It was always booked solid and attracted a diversified class of refined people, she said.

"And, boy are you lucky," she insisted. "This summer's cruise has an unusually large group of professional single men. "And such a reasonable price," she cooed as she slid the charge slip across the table for us to sign.

Total cost, by the time you included off-shore health and Bermuda Triangle insurance, paid-in-advance 20 percent gratuities, seasickness shots and other incidentals, came to $4,550.23 each, which entitled us to Meal Plan A—all the grub we could eat and wine spritzers with every meal, including breakfast.

It wasn't until we were well out to sea that

we discovered everyone else paid less and got more, and that the single scene on the ocean was as bad as it was on land. Worse, actually, because you couldn't leave and take a cab home.

The agent didn't lie about the available professional men, though. There were about 200 of them (average height four-foot-four), otherwise known as the crew. These guys would pop up at every opportunity with offers of food, drink, and other services, which they would have been happy to demonstrate if we accompanied them on a romantic stroll of the crew deck—a portholeless pit at the base of the ship into which several women ventured and were never seen again.

The badgering finally got so bad, I went to the captain. This dapper gentleman explained such behavior was innate to the European male psyche, a fact he could elaborate on if I were to meet him in the lifeboat on deck two at sunset, where we could share his personal stash of Asti Spumanti imported from Australia, where the girls were "bella," "bella," but could never hold a candle to "bella," "bella" me.

I told him I'd rather jump overboard.

Of course, there were plenty of other engaging activities for single women, including one very popular water sport. This event took place at pool side where the Director of Entertainment, a toupeed man in a Speedo bathing suit with a healthy overhang of stomach, would gather zaftig ladies wearing thong bikinis and more jewelry than the queen on Coronation Day.

After handing them a free, white, thin-as-one-ply toilet paper T-shirt to put on, this aging Master of Ceremonies would select a noticeably enthusiastic single guy (who invariably had hair growing on his shoulders and blemishes on his back) to throw cold water on the upper half of the challengers' torsos. Onlookers would then applaud and the woman who got the loudest cheers won a magnum of champagne bottled in Brooklyn, which she and the guy who doused her presumably would drink together that night as they swapped numbers and anti-acne remedies.

On a scale of one to ten, that particular year's jaunt got a minus three. The only plus was the free week I won to some place called Camp Swingaway in the Berkshires, which I immediately sold to a woman from New Jersey for $1,000 and a free canvas bag with a "Kiss" logo.

So, yes, for me, marriage makes summertime twice as sweet. I can relax without that sense of urgency. Do I miss it? The anticipation? The chase? The thrill of a new romance? The throbbing hangovers?

Ah, no. What's more, come June and July, when I see my neighbor's daughter and her single girlfriends drive away in a convertible, headed for the nightlife in the Hamptons, the Jersey Shore, or Martha's Vineyard, I can smile and wave them on.

"Good luck, girls," I say under my breath and wave. "You're gonna need it."

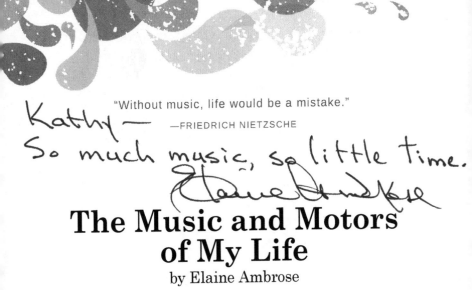

"Without music, life would be a mistake."

—FRIEDRICH NIETZSCHE

Kathy —
So much music, so little time.
Elaine Ambrose

The Music and Motors of My Life

by Elaine Ambrose

Music remains an important part of my life. And I intend to keep it that way until I'm too old to sing Middle C. I relate favorite songs with decades of driving, and every car I've owned has contributed to my personal and passionate playlist. Here are a few:

1966. I was 14, a frizzy-haired, nearsighted freshman in high school. He was 18, a senior athlete and hard-working farm boy. My parents had approved of our friendship because we attended the same church youth group. One night after the football game, he drove me home in his father's cattle truck. I was as nervous as a squirrel in the middle of a busy road.

Just then, a Beatles' song "We Can Work It Out" started to play on the radio. Now, I loved The Beatles. But my dad didn't. He'd been in a perpetual bad mood for two years since Barry Goldwater lost the presidential election. So I had to hide my Beatles 45s as if they were contraband. Then, late at night, I'd secretly listen to them in my room, in my pjs, with my hair curled around empty orange juice cans—a futile attempt to straighten it.

I knew all sorts of Beatles trivia as well.

"Did you know," I said to my date, whom I had secretly named Senior Stud Muffin, "this song was written by Paul McCartney and John Lennon, but George Harrison changed the middle verse to make it three-quarter time like a waltz?"

Senior Stud Muffin wasn't interested in my musical expertise. He was too busy attempting to hug and kiss me. My thoughts still on the music, I wasn't prepared for his advances. My brain was momentarily absent without leave. When I snapped out of it, I lunged toward him smack into the solid gear shift between the seats. The shock and pain caused me to let out a yelp. Seconds later, the porch light turned on; my father stood by the screen. The mood was ruined.

I opened the heavy door of the cattle truck and hopped down to the ground.

Senior Stud Muffin yanked the truck into first gear and sped away without so much as a "Thanks" or "See you later." I walked into the house, thinking we probably couldn't have worked it out anyway.

1973. My first car was a '73, candy-apple red, Pontiac Firebird. My father gave it to me for my pending college graduation. After the humiliating experience in the cattle truck, I focused on new techniques for maneuvering around the gear shift so I could canoodle with my new boyfriend, a soulful musician I named Adagio, for various reasons.

We broke up that spring. But I didn't care because I still had my car. After graduation, I loaded all my worldly possessions into the Firebird: a metal trunk full of clothes, a few boxes of books and term papers, my hot rollers, and my $25 guitar from Sears. I inserted a Carly Simon cartridge into the car's eight-track tape player and drove away from the University of Idaho with the idealistic enthusiasm of a 21-year-old woman who had no debt, no boyfriend, and no job. I felt liberated.

Reality brought my Firebird freedom days to an end. I started a full-time job, got married, and had to part with my car. My husband, a good and efficient man I called Sparky, and I made a total of $1,000 a month between us. So we bought a sensible Mercury Comet with no radio and shared it. The car was brown. I was blue. When I drove it, I sang sad songs, out of tune, and out of luck.

1978. I saved enough money to buy my own car—a bright-yellow Volkswagen Super Beetle with an AM-FM radio. I drove to work singing "Dancing Queen" by ABBA. The interior became too small after I got pregnant and couldn't fit behind the wheel. The next upgrade was a white Pontiac Phoenix—with a car seat and a cassette player full of lullabies.

1980. After the second child, we simply had to purchase a Ford Bronco because we needed room for "stuff," including a case of Girl Scout cookies just for me. Working full-time, caring for two small children, and balancing home and marriage altered my musical repertoire. I often focused on survival, and the top tune of the day was a duet with Barbra Streisand and Donna Summer singing "No More Tears" ("Enough is Enough").

1991. Near my 40th birthday, I bought a Pontiac Grand Prix touring car. I drove it happily while I belted out Billy Joel's "We Didn't Start the Fire" and "I'm Your Baby Tonight" by Whitney Houston. Then, one day, the music stopped. An irresponsible punk ran a stop sign and smashed into me. I woke up in the hospital with broken bones, cracked ribs, and serious nerve damage to the back of my head. The loser wasn't injured and skipped town. My car was a total loss. I returned to singing the blues.

2000s. Now the kids are grown and gone, and my vehicle is a sturdy SUV. I have a CD player and a port for the playlists from my iPhone. My other favorite necessity is an air conditioner, which comes in handy to tame hot flashes. I haven't used a stick shift in decades, and even though I have a new husband I fondly call Studley, the only steam on my windows is caused by going through the automatic car wash.

Sometimes, though, when traffic is light and the roads are clear, I'll turn on some '70s music and take a long drive. I'll remember that feisty college graduate who was eager for the open highway and didn't have a care in the world. I'll sing along with The Beatles on their long and winding road and end with a grateful salute to the Bee Gees because I'm still "stayin' alive."

*To Kathy,
Lisa Marlin
#madonna rocks
#Kathyrockstoo*

Madonna Wannabe
by Lisa Marlin

The best thing about being in my twenties in the '80s is that social media didn't exist. Mark Zuckerberg wouldn't launch Facebook from his Harvard dorm until 2004. By then, I was a mature mother of four, who carefully chose the words and photos that would be most appropriate, and least incriminating, to share with the online world.

But if we had social media back then, in my college years, that wouldn't have been the case. And then, today, my kids would have evidence as to why I'm not fit to judge their unwise choices.

"But look, Mom," they'd say, pointing to an old photo of me and my college roommate on their phones. "Here's a post from 1985. Check out your eyes; they're bloodshot and glassy. What was that all about?" What's more, they'd demand to know what I meant by my status: "I'm like a virgin! #madonnarocks."

So I'd have to explain. I'd have to tell them my eyes were reacting to second-hand smoke. That there weren't any smoking bans back then, and people could light up in restaurants and even on airplanes, enticed to do so by television commercials and highway billboards. The Marlboro Man, I'd have to point out, with his rugged cowboy good looks and cigarette dangling from his mouth as he wrangled cattle, made it sexy to smoke. So lots of people did, wherever they went.

"I was at the mercy of my environs," I'd have to admit to the kids. "We all were. Everyone had red eyes in the '80s." Sounds logical, no? My kids wouldn't think anything of it. After all, they weren't there.

As for my status on my hypothetical post, I'd tell them that friends and I had gone to see mega-pop star Madonna perform at the Frank Erwin Center on the University of Texas campus. It was one of the stops during her debut concert called "The Virgin Tour." Hence my virgin reference.

"We were lucky to have scored tickets," I'd tell them.

Perhaps I could explain away one social media post from my life in the '80s. But what if I would've tweeted a photo of my bestie and I dressed like street walkers on Halloween? Not sure I could justify now why I thought that had been a good idea then.

Come to think of it, it may not have even been Halloween. It could have just been a hot summer night in the city. No matter, with its hip bars and live music, Sixth Street was (and still is) the coolest scene in Austin. And we wanted to be seen there...often. That is, when we could catch a break from college homework and shifts at our jobs at the steakhouse. I remember that after work we'd change from our polyester waitress uniforms into leather miniskirts, off-the-shoulder neon T-shirts, big bangle earrings, and high heels. Then we'd hit the party street like the Madonna-wannabes we were.

We knew exactly what to wear and how to act because, since 1981, we had our MTV. We could finally toss out the magazines that we'd counted on for fashion advice through the '70s. Instead, we could turn the knob on the front of our boxed television sets to the cable channel that broadcast music videos 24-7. Within minutes, we'd know the latest styles any time of the day, or night.

From watching Madonna, Whitney Houston, and Cyndi Lauper, we knew we could be the girls who just wanted to have fun while we strutted our stuff in big hair, leg warmers pulled over our high-waisted jeans, and shoulder pads stitched into our shirts. Thanks to Rick Springfield, Journey, and Michael Jackson, we knew that guys with mullet haircuts, who wore skin-tight pants and flipped-up shirt collars were bad, in a very good way for us, of course.

It was mostly all good back then—the fashion, the music, my behavior. And what makes it even better in my memory is that none of it was ever being recorded into infinity. I thank my lucky star that there isn't an Instagram story from that Madonna concert.

If I'd have had the opportunity then, I'd have made a selfie video of my friend and I screaming at the top of our lungs when Madonna broke into the lyrics of her hit song, "Like a Virgin." It didn't matter if we knew what that meant. We sang along like it was written for us, anyway, swaying dizzily from all the various aromas swirling through the auditorium. It's a fun memory for me. But not one I'd want my kids to come across unexpectedly in an online search.

Same goes for the milk crates we used to steal in the middle of the night from behind the neighborhood grocery store. We used them as shelves in our tiny apartments back them. If I'd have been able to, I might have put a picture on Pinterest of those crates that we artistically stacked and filled with photos, candles stuck in the tops of empty wine bottles, and various decorative beads and bangles. Since I couldn't post it then, there's really no need to confess to the crate caper now.

Being in my twenties in the '80s, before social media came along and changed the way the world communicates and remembers, was a stroke of good timing for me. So there is no proof that I lived anything but a respectable life, always making wise choices.

In the eyes of my children, my past remains untainted. In the words of a status that never made it online, I'm like a virgin. And I couldn't be happier.

> "We are all here for a spell;
> get all the good laughs you can."
> —WILL ROGERS

To Kathy:
Kaye Curren
2018

What a Way to Go
by Kaye Curren

It's not the cheeriest of things to think about. But I'm of an age to consider it: my end and how I'll dispose of myself. Back and forth in my mind— burial or cremation? Cremation or burial? Which is less barbaric? Which hurts the least? (Though I guess being dead renders that point moot.) To burn or to rot?—that is the question.

In an attempt to figure out which way to go, I looked back on two family ceremonies to see what they could teach me.

Mom's funeral was one of them. She was of the generation before cremation became popular. So my sister, Jane, and I decided on a traditional burial. Of course, casket shopping was first on the list, and we bought Mom an amazing one. It was porcelain, with painted wildflowers in pink and yellow woven among green vines. It was lined in the softest pink velvet. I remember we were quite impressed.

"It certainly looks comfy," Jane said, running her fingers over the lining.

I agreed.

The funeral director jumped on the opportunity.

"Try it," he said, seriously. And we did.

Afterwards, despite the cost, we both made a quick decision: "We'll take it."

The ceremony itself was a hit from the poetic eulogy by our brother to a rousing rendition of "Amazing Grace." The casket, however, was the star. And that made Jane and I embarrassed, since relatives and friends spoke of nothing else.

"That casket!" Aunt Barb yelled at me in the vestibule after the service. "Where did you get it? I need one just like it," she said excitedly. Now, generally, if Aunt Barb registered an emotion above "My, my," we called the medics immediately. So her enthusiasm for our choice, as well as the approval from the other mourners, made me grateful we hadn't gone for the plain wooden box.

"Check with Jane, Aunt Barb," I said, as I gave her a hug. "She'll hook you up."

My mother's service was a quiet, beautiful affair, nice music, no major gaffes or family crises.

What's more, we received a lovely note from the funeral director, thanking us for the dozens of inquiries he received for special-order caskets.

My ex-husband John's service, on the other hand, was a different story. By then, cremation had become *de rigueur*, and John's children wanted to honor his wishes. So cremation it was.

I was a bunch of nerves when I walked into the memorial. "The Girlfriend," my ex-husband's latest, had been placed in charge of the affair, and she was not overly fond of me. Since the event was held in John's favorite honky-tonk hotel, I wore bright red cowboy boots as a hat tip to the memory of our horse-riding days. I knew my daughters would appreciate the fun of it. How much this was a dig to The Girlfriend, I'm not prepared to say.

When The Girlfriend arrived, she took one look at the boots, made a face, then breezed past me without a word. So, there we were: The Girlfriend, two daughters, two stepdaughters, five grandchildren, assorted relatives and friends, and me.

I had no experience with cremation. We had traditional burials for my parents, and, thankfully, other deceased relatives and friends had kept their ashes to themselves. So you can imagine my surprise when John's daughter, Susan, his second child from his first marriage, bounded into the hotel room with a large cardboard box, from which she took several Ziploc lunch baggies and plunked them on the table.

"Here's Daddy!" she announced with a smile. "Let us begin."

We all stood in silence, wide-eyed, staring at the baggies. My mouth dropped. My two daughters' eyes rolled. And a few mourners whipped out their cell phones to text and take photos. The Girlfriend, who insisted on standing for the whole service, sighed, clutched at her heart, and leaned on a nearby wall for support.

Thankfully, the slideshow of John's life began, and we could focus on reveries and loving remarks by family members. Yet I couldn't quite grasp that the remains of the man I had married and then befriended for 30 years lay naked and powdery in see-through lunch bags right in front of me. As we all wept and offered each other tissues, I found myself thinking about him in a rather macabre way:

Was that his hand in that baggie—the hand that lovingly pitched hay for the horses? And over there, was that bag filled with the same foot that shooed away the neighbor's cat from our door? How about the ears that never seemed to hear it was time to do the dishes—were they in the small baggie on the left?

Later, as the tiny cremation parcels were passed out to the elect, myself excluded, I thought,

Thank God. See you in the hereafter, John, where I hope you have all your parts. Then, I quietly left the building.

Looking back, my ex-husband's memorial clinched it: No cremation for me. The idea of having my feet, hands, or any part of my body poured into transparent Ziplocs and handed out to funeral-goers is totally abhorrent to me. What's more, having my remains fall into the hands of certain relatives I couldn't stand when I was in the flesh makes my skin crawl.

So burial it is. Traditional. The whole nine yards.

But I want one heck of a casket, like Mom's. Gorgeous. Porcelain, with ceramic roses all over it. And lined with the softest pink velvet.

Better than a baggie any day.

Breathless Encounter
by Fritzy Dean

My grandmother owned a mysterious garment call a corset. It was a rigid, laced contraption with strong stays, which held her erect and gave her a shapely figure. I remember she needed help to get into it, and when it was finally in place, she could hardly breathe.

Thinking back, I suspect those corsets were the main reason so many women had several "fainting couches" around the house. Wearing these tightly bound contraptions may have made these lovelies look more alluring. But not getting the proper oxygen made them lightheaded. So they probably needed a convenient place to swoon.

I, myself, a modern woman, remember wearing what was known as a panty girdle. It was miles from being a panty, but was deemed essential if you wanted to look thinner than you really were. It did what the corset was meant to do, only with less force, and for different body parts. Like the corset, it took effort to get into. It also required a good deal of yanking to keep it from riding up like a delinquent window shade. Years passed. I became a feminist, and although I didn't burn my bra, I did happily consign my panty girdle to the trash can.

More years passed. I grew lumpy and jiggly. And while this wasn't the worst thing in the world, when I read something about an undergarment called a "shaper," my curiosity got the better of me. On that rare day when I found myself in a mall store, I decided to see for myself. So I walked over to the lingerie department to investigate.

Oh, my! Where to begin? Such a range of choices: There were all-in-one body shapers, waist-to-toe shapers, tummy-trimming shapers, waist-and-thigh shapers, and one called a camisole shaper. That one intrigued me enough to pick the largest size and take it to the dressing room. It looked the least uncomfortable. It was just a wisp of a thing, but long enough, I figured, to smooth my muffin top and flatten my back Jello.

Alone in the biggest fitting room I could find, I confidently slipped off my shirt and slipped into the camisole. Well, actually, that's not true. I wasn't able to just slither into it. That little piece of clothing had the tensile strength of knitted steel. First, I tugged one side, then the other, then the front, and then the back—and then repeat, repeat, repeat. Sweating heavily, I finally got the shaper on. I wanted to look at my new image in the mirror, but, instead, I was gasping for air. *Where's a fainting couch when you need one?* I thought.

"That's it," I said partly scared, partly annoyed. "I'm too old and too smart for this kind of torture." And then I prayed: "Lord, help me get this thing off and I'll always be satisfied with the way I look. Promise. Amen."

I tried pulling the shaper over my head the way I had put it on. The fabric, thin and stretchy, rolled in on itself and formed a chokingly tight band diagonally across my body. I tried poking one arm out. I got it through up to the elbow, but it would go no farther. So, now, with my right arm stuck, I tried working one-handed to pull, push, and inch my way out of the thing.

Like quicksand, the more I struggled, the more I became encased. I tried one more time, but no luck. My mind raced. I peeked out the door. None of the salesgirls looked strong enough to free me. So I imagined the worst-case scenario. I'd have to call 911—that's if I could even reach my cell phone. In my frazzled, frenzied state, I thought about the conversation:

911: *What is your emergency?*

Me: *Help! I'm trapped!*

911: *Can you give us your location?*

Me: *Trapped, I tell you! And I can't breathe!*

911: *Do you need the Jaws of Life? Where are you?*

Me: *I'm in a shaper...in a dressing room at Kohls. And I'm running out of oxygen. Help!*

What a ridiculous exchange. I couldn't go there, even in my head. But just the thought gave me the burst of adrenaline I needed. I pulled my arm free and wrenched that boa constrictor camisole down to my waist, down over my hips, down my thighs and finally, with a thrust that almost knocked me over, I kicked the shaper off my foot. I collapsed onto the bench, taking in a big gulp of air, and thanked the Lord. Free at last!

When I got my strength back, I dressed, all the while muttering how I'd probably have to buy the stupid shaper because I'd stretched it out so much only a rhino could wear it. But guess what? I picked that silly thing up, put it on its dainty little hanger, and watched in amazement as it snapped itself back to its original Barbie doll size. Scary.

All my sweaty struggles, all my pulling and yanking, all the effort it took to get it on and off, indeed, all the nasty words I had called it—nothing had changed that sucker. Its perky, teeny, tiny take-your-breath-away shape remained intact.

Gratefully, I hung it on the rack by the door, waited until the coast was clear, then made my getaway.

As I hurried out of the store, I vowed that nothing would ever take my breath away again. What's more, I learned an important life lesson: There is absolutely nothing wrong with lumps and jiggles. I am fine exactly as I am.

A Picture Is Worth a Thousand Words

by Anne Elise O'Connor

Women spend the better part of our adult lives taking care of others—kids, husbands, hairdressers. But at some point, we realize it's our time to shine.

This realization might come when the final kid gets his college diploma. It suddenly hits us that we've graduated, too. We've accomplished all the "shoulds" in our life and can now start conquering all our "wants."

Or, as what happened in my case, it could strike when we notice hubby is checking out the same hard-bodied lifeguard at the beach as we are. That's just the kick in the pants we might need to give our dutiful gay husband his walking papers. And that's exactly what I did.

Okay, I'll admit my "cute-young-thing" days are over. But there's still life in me yet. So, I figured it was time to let loose and see what I missed while being a responsible adult.

My 60-plus dating adventures began where many ill-fated ideas do: on the internet. I checked out some bios on "Let's Connect," and tentatively responded to a few. But, after weeks of tedious flirting, nothing came of it. So I decided to take control. As a former public relations professional, I had planned marketing campaigns before. The only difference, now, was I'd be marketing myself.

I wrote an ad I thought showed I was intelligent, witty, and adventurous. I ran it by four friends, made some tweaks, and posted it online. No photos. I'd been advised that can be dangerous—especially for women. Apparently, pictures bring out the weirdos and the creeps.

Still, though I wasn't about to share what I looked like initially, I did want to see how handsome (or not) my prospects were. So I ended my ad by writing that responses with pictures would be answered first, and if I replied, I'd attach a photo. Filled with the kind of butterflies you get from anticipating an exciting experience, I hit the send button.

That night, I dreamed of hot-air balloon rides

over the Sonoma vineyards, scuba diving at the Great Barrier Reef, and insightful discussions about current events over Sunday brunch.

The next day, I couldn't wait to get online. I was thrilled when I saw I had 63 new messages. I skipped over those without attachments and clicked on the first one that had a photo.

It was a picture of a penis. I received penis pictures from 37 different men.

Now, I'm as big a fan of penises as any heterosexual female. But let's face it—they are not that photogenic. What's more, what a man's private parts look like is not the first thing I need to know about a potential date.

But I persevered.

After deleting the 37 penis shots, I scrolled through the 26 emails of men who sent me pictures of themselves above their necks. And I actually went out with a few. Many were nice, normal, intelligent men. Boring.

Then there were others. Like the seemingly intelligent engineer whose idea of appropriate first-date conversation was to ask if I had "ever had cuffs slapped on me." He was sincerely disappointed when I fluttered my eyes and told him truthfully I'd never been arrested.

Another piece of advice I got from friends was to always meet in a public place. I chose the quiet bar of a mid-priced fish-and-steak restaurant. It was a couple of miles from my home and close to a major highway—perfect for quick getaways.

Since I viewed this experiment as a marketing campaign, I wanted to collect as much data as possible in the shortest amount of time. So I scheduled multiple wine dates that would allow me to meet seven men face-to-face and give me free nights for follow-up dinners with the promising ones.

Week one had both high and low moments. One guy was so creepy, he could have stepped out of a zombie apocalypse movie. So I took a sip of wine, excused myself, headed for the restroom, detoured, and bolted. The second man was nice, but there were no sparks so I declined another date with him. The third gentleman was funny, had a good job, and said he liked cats. When he asked to see me for dinner the following week, I happily accepted.

I had the second date with the cat lover and felt definite potential there. Still, I was scheduled to meet three more men. So I told him I'd be in touch. My cup runneth over, so I could afford to be choosy.

The next night I was back at the bar for my fourth online dating encounter. As I sat down, the bartender greeted me with a wink. "What'll it be? Your regular?" he asked, leaning in. I was mortified! In less than two weeks, I'd become a barfly. This was not how my mother raised her daughter to behave.

Number five arrived shortly after, and the evening got better. We talked and laughed for almost two hours. Thoughts of *this could be the one* floated through my mind. When he asked to see me the following Thursday, I couldn't say "yes," fast enough. He walked me to my car and then lingered.

"Wait," he cooed. "I've a little present for you." Number five ran to his car and came back with a small, brightly wrapped gift bag. He put on a big smile as he handed it to me.

"Will you wear these every day until we see each other again?" he asked, seriously. When I stared at him blankly, he added, "Then I can take them home and have the sweet smell of you wherever I go. So don't bother washing them. Okay?"

He was a sock sniffer. I had heard they existed. But until now, I'd never met one.

That did it for me. I decided the universe was saying it's time to shut down this find-a-man marketing campaign...for the time being, at least. I'm not a quitter, though. So, I'll do some more research and regroup.

I'm sure there's a way to write an ad stating penis picture-takers, handcuff aficionados, and sock sniffers need not apply. So when I find the right formula, I'll be back online searching for Mr. Right.

*"I have neither the time, nor the crayons,
to explain this to you."*

—PINTEREST

The New Millennium Office

by Barbara L. Smith

Let's face it: The workplace these days belongs to the young. I discovered this the first day I reported for full-time work after years of freelance writing.

When I was introduced to Ashley, Kaylee, Josh, and Jaden, I knew my days with Dick and Jane were far behind. Maria, a contemporary who had hired me, abandoned ship soon after I was "welcomed aboard." So there I was, the only member of the in-house ad agency wearing bifocals and taking cholesterol drugs.

The new boss and head of creative, Zach, was under thirty, and more than three decades my junior. Top management hired him to reflect a funkier, Facebook/Twitter/Snapchat/LinkedIn/ Pinterest image. Thus, from the start, I was on foreign soil—a new horizon I was not familiar with—one that required multi-energy, multi-tasking, and multi-thinking, multis I hadn't used in years.

The "kids" (my co-workers) arrived early and worked late. Afterwards, they'd go out clubbing, down Mojitos by the pitcher, and collect business cards. Next day, though, they were bright, chirpy, and at their desks before the sun came up. I struggled to make it in by 9:15, and at 5 o'clock, after eight hours on the job, I knew where I wanted to be—on the parkway heading home to green tea and a good book.

So, one evening about eight, the phone rang. It was Zach who was, natch, still in the office. I was in my slippers.

"Hey, Barb. How are ya?"

"I'm watching "The Bachelor.""

"I got great news," he said, all fired up. "We got the green light for Kidzilla."

After a long silence from me, he said. "Remember, I told you they might partner with us on the new campaign?" I did remember, though Zach probably thought, at my age, I'd forgotten who I was even talking to.

"Kidzilla is in your face," he ranted on.

"Their sneaks rock. Can you scratch up some ideas for a 'present' tomorrow? Our audience is 'tweens and teens,' so think Katy Perry not Tony Bennett." Zach couldn't see me, but I was rolling my eyes.

"And guess what else?" he said.

I couldn't even imagine.

"For a celebrity promo, we're trying to line up Justin Bieber. He's, like, a red-hot 'get.' It would be like Jimmy Kimmel getting Vladimir Putin for a 'sit-down,'" he said.

"I'll sleep on it, Zach," I said.

"No can do," he persisted. "I need some ideas now, esta noche, like, tonight."

"It's after eight," I protested.

"So?" he said with innocence. "Kidzilla's people are coming in at ten. We have to have something by then."

"Seriously?" I asked again.

"If you can get back to me by midnight, I can shoot your stuff over to Matt, and he can take it and whip up some graphics. I'm counting on you, Barb, Barbie," he said, and hung up.

Well, I clicked off "The Bachelor" and clicked on the coffeemaker. I needed to show Zach that my mind was not as ancient as my body. Hyped up on enough caffeine to make a dozen Starbucks' grande macchiatos, I pulled together some passable stuff. I got those to Zach and, though I was exhausted the next morning, we were ready for Kidzilla. I was a hero.

Things went well for a while. But just when I thought I was on top of things, Zach called me in for a chat.

"The 'suits' want to do some repositioning," he began. I suspected I was the one being repositioned.

"We're not taking full advantage of the new media," he said. "From now on, we're going full throttle on the Web."

"I don't do Web writing," I said truthfully.

"Barb, Barbie," Zach said, pacing his office like an expectant father. "Times have changed. The Net's where it's at."

"I write promotional brochures and print ads," I said blankly.

"Print is last year. Last decade. Last century. No one reads newspapers and magazines anymore. At least nobody I know," said Zach.

All the while, I kept thinking: *Does anyone he knows even read?*

"We're going YouTube. We wanna get ads on Google's home page. We need to jump on analytics. We need SEO." Zach could hardly contain himself.

"What's SEO?" I asked him.

"Barbie, Barbie, you gotta get better connected," Zach insisted. "Log on. Scroll around. Take a look at what's out there. You'll get some ideas."

As if I didn't have any ideas already. But my ideas apparently reeked of Lipitor. I knew I was out of touch in the new millennium office. Soon, I suspected, I would go the way of the typewriter and the floppy disk. Soon I'd be sent out to pasture like an old retired nag.

"Grab a quick yogurt," Zach insisted. "Josh and I are scoping out the competition at the mall. Tag along. I'll drive."

Actually, I didn't want to go to the mall. I didn't want to tag along.

"Love to," I said. "I'll meet you out front."

Zach drove a truck and I didn't want to ride in the "bed." But when I called "shotgun!" he and Josh looked at each other like I had finally lost it. Neither one of them knew what I was talking about. So I covered my mouth and feigned a sneeze.

To my credit, I hung on at the job for five years. To the end, I remained a team player. I learned a lot about youth and Zach and Ashley and Josh. They were exceptional kids. They were extremely talented. They could adapt with a second's notice.

As for me, at that point, I realized I didn't want to be a part of this fast-talk, fast-think kid nation any longer. I wanted to spend more time with other people on adult meds. So I said "so long," and put myself out to pasture. And, trust me. I'm much happier out there with the old gray mares.

Freezing My Assets Off
by DC Stanfa

One day I looked in the mirror and about fell through it, like Alice, attempting to stop the evil clock, Lord of Time. The encouraging phrase, "keep your chin up" came to mind, while the cynical caterpillar in my head answered, "That's easier when you only have one."

By the time I turned fifty, I was up three pant sizes and had the energy level of a bivalve mollusk. I was NOT happy as a clam. Skinny girls never see fat and fifty in their futures. We are attacked from our behinds. My behind snuck up while I sat working, writing, and driving. Writer's butt and driver's butt conspired and gave me a colossal Kardashian backside. I stopped running because I couldn't fit into my shorts, and realized my husband stopped trying to get into them, too—mostly for the same reason.

Our move to Florida, when I turned fifty-five, at least got me off the couch. In Ohio, before the move, I'd exhumed the contents of my gym locker. The autopsy concluded that my racquetball career died from a kill shot in 1999. My yoga mat namasted away in 2004.

The neighborhood bike rides were liberating in the Sunshine State, but I was pushing into a plus size and not peddling fast enough to catch myself. It was going to take a lot more to unbake my rolls.

My favorite hobby of wine drinking on our dock built a shelf underneath the size 36 C rack I'd installed decades earlier. Clearly, that investment was expanding with age. My upper abs were growing "flab"ulous and my belly had a Cinnabon in the oven. Apparently, I loved wine and chocolate more than I hated my love handles. They were growing with mutual affection. Party on, Girth.

The "change" is not a currency you can really cash in on. On the contrary, subsequent "procedures" are expensive. When women develop the midlife middle, I believe we should all throw celebratory showers for the baby-less bump. No need to determine how many TP squares it takes to measure-the-girth game. Instead, we should be surrounded by our middle-aged female family and friends, and cascaded with love and reassurance. Think open bar, wholesale Botox, and liposuction Groupons.

My other menopause symptoms were a hot flash in the pan compared to the weight gain. My mood swings were mild. I only went from Jekyll to Hyde, bursting at the seams and throwing fits—when the pants didn't. My insomnia was irritating, but tossing and turning was the only exercise program I had.

While hormone therapy would possibly help with metabolism and weight loss, it was just as likely to bring my libido back. What if I didn't lose weight? What if I was just hefty and horny? Surely that'd be karma for my past sins. Perhaps every time I had my bell rung, angels didn't get wings but I added a future layer of fat, like rings on a tree—a cumulative demerit system where the digits ganged up and knocked me off my Toledo scale.

I considered a tummy tuck and liposuction. Then I heard about CoolSculpting, a non-invasive fat-freezing procedure that targets exercise-resistant areas on the body. Considering my entire body was exercise-resistant, I thought I might be a good candidate/spokesmodel: Puffy The Midlife Draggin'.

Hillary, the nurse performing the CoolSculpting, was very thorough and precise, explaining what to expect, including discomfort during the initial suction cup placement; bruising, swelling and other possible complications in the weeks following. She neglected to warn me about the mordant "before" photography session, in which I nearly fainted from trauma. I was flubbergasted.

The initial suction of the CruelSculpting machine felt like it was trying to harvest my organs, one at a time. Hillary truly comforted me (holding my hand) despite her being a size zero. While my blubber processed into fatsicles, I lamented my decade-long laziness: What happened to that girl who loved to dance? And where are her cheekbones?

I went off to find her. I started on a 1,300-calorie-a-day diet and picked up the pace on the bike. On inclement days, I walked. It was a long road, but a short trip from booty calls to walking malls.

I began bio-identical hormone replacement choosing to embrace whichever me showed up as a result—skinny, horny, neither or both.

The CoolSculpting un-crusted my Chardonnay soufflé, which motivated me to stay the diet and exercise course. I also stalked old high school friends' pictures on Facebook. Were we all in the same bloat? Verdict: No more teenage waistband, except for Cindy, who'd apparently subsisted on kale and quinoa—never once contemplating cheesecake.

I cut out all fried foods, white foods, pizza-foods, and desserts. I checked the calories in everything, including toothpaste and toothpicks. Despite the diet, and averaging 5,000 steps a day on my health-tracker, I worried that the evil digits wouldn't go down without more of a fight.

When traveling, my only option was airport food. I'd max-out my daily calories before customer dinners (where I'd push salad greens around with my fork). Just how many calories did that little exercise burn?

I was finally down a pant size, but fed up about not being properly fed.

During one mall walk, I encountered a sample pusher holding suckers in front of the See's Candy store.

"How many calories?" I inquired.

"Eighty," she answered.

I was sucked in like the camera to Giada's De Laurentis's cleavage. I walked for twenty minutes, licking away one quarter of the candy. I rewrapped it and kept it in my car, where I sucked it a little more, slowly for weeks. I told my daughter about this when she came to visit, while we walked the same mall.

"What a sad story, Mom. That's how Charlie ate his birthday Wonka Bar," she said.

Her words were my golden ticket to kicking the Charlie-and-his-chocolate-factory-bucket-diet to the curb.

Cry me a chocolate river, and call me Augustus Gloop.

> "When my kids become wild and unruly,
> I use a nice, safe playpen. When they're finished,
> I climb out."
>
> —ERMA BOMBECK

I Don't Want to Be a Mommy

by Allia Zobel Nolan

Isn't it always the way—people you hardly know ask the most personal questions. I have a ring on my finger, so the "What, no husband yet?" has finally stopped. Now, strangers stare at my stomach and inquire "Any babies yet?" I have a pat answer for this intrusion. "Ah, no," I murmur in a low tone and look gravely. "There's insanity in the family."

Time was when a woman of my tender years could have said, "Get real. I'm too old," and that would be that. Today, though, it seems nothing's impossible. Like a bad science fiction movie, real-life doctors are fertilizing eggs in everything but a martini shaker, and implanting them in females of all ages—even those on Medicare. As a result, women old enough for life alert and Polident are becoming mothers for the first time, (some even having their own grandchildren). I give these women credit. Anyone who can manage a walker and a stroller deserves a toast—Ensure, of course, because she's going to need it.

At any age, becoming a mommy isn't something a woman does just because she can. Choosing motherhood is the single most important decision a female can make, one most women don't take lightly, given the commitment it involves.

It takes a special person to be a "Mom." She has to be loving, understanding, self-sacrificing, brave, and have a good sense of humor. She must be as patient as Job, know as much as Google, and be as generous as a Political Action Committee in an election year. Moms have to be nurses, chauffeurs, seamstresses, teachers, cooks, and friends. They have to have a cache of money stashed away for frequent emergencies, and keep a spare bed always at the ready. In short, Moms have to be superheroes. Most (like yours and mine) are all that and more.

Still, not every female is cut out to be a mom. And I think it's the smart woman who recognizes this. Take me, for instance. When God handed out maternal instinct, He gave it all to my sister, (who—honest to goodness—has 12 children). I figured this out early on because while other kids were playing with dolls, I was writing poems about them: "Mary's baby has one blue eye; the other eye fell out. Mary ate it yesterday on a roll with sauerkraut."

Don't get me wrong. I love kids. It's just that circumstances weren't right for me to have them. (I did get plenty of offers from donors, though. Unfortunately, none of them was affiliated with any sperm banks.) And now that my situation has changed, I don't think I could, or that I really want to, balance deadlines and diapers, colic and bursitis.

Some psychologists contend women need to have children to feel complete, except if they're creative in other ways, because the creativity fills the gap in their inner spaces. I think it's fat (or cats?)—not writing—that's filled my gap. But then, I've never put much stock in such mumbo-jumbo anyway.

Still, thoughts of being a mommy did cross my mind once. It was at the park and my girlfriend was playing with her daughter. The little girl laughed, gave her mom a huge hug, and I felt a sudden pang (which turned out to be gas from a garlic pickle I ate at lunch). Later, my friend wanted to leave, but her daughter didn't. At this, the little cherub kicked her mom in the knee and ran into the playground where a swing hit her in the head leaving us to race madly to the emergency room where the youngster got eleven stitches, bit the resident trying to give her a tetanus shot and, after letting out a screech that'd curl iron, threw up all over him.

This episode cleared my head, and at the same time reinforced my belief that it takes a special person to be a mommy—someone younger, with a stronger heart and a better stomach.

Nevertheless, I have to say, though I wasn't cut out to be one, Moms are super people. And after all, where would we be without them?

*To Kathy —
Amy Abbott*

Bonfire of the Inanities

by Amy McVay Abbott

My husband and I are nose-to-nose with a lifetime of personal effects spread throughout a house too large for two. We both agree: It's time for something smaller, a home with less maintenance. And less junk. Looking back, I can barely piece together how we acquired, and why we continue to hold on to, all this stuff.

We moved to our first house three weeks before our son arrived. I finally had room for my most prized possession, a maple spinet piano. We had a two-car garage—space for a lawn mower, leaf blower, Craftsman tools.

Of course, the baby had his own things. Besides his umbrella stroller, high chair, Pack and Play, walker, playpen, and Bouncy seat, he had electric trains, Beanie Babies, Lego creations and Teenage Mutant Ninja Turtles. Trip on a Lincoln Log nightly for a few years, and it's time for a toy room. We needed to move.

With our new house, we doubled the square footage, complete with a playroom, basement foosball, and air hockey tables. Paradise found for a child with a hundred million unmatched Lego pieces. We also had a guest room, a family room, a closet just for the ugly green Samsonite luggage from 1975 high school graduations. More stuff, sprouting like unfettered dandelions in spring.

Fast forward to today, and our space seems overwhelming. Our son lives his grown-up life a thousand miles away. Our pets have died. The now-vintage spinet, where two generations of non-musicians fingered unholy interpretations of Bach preludes, glows like toxic waste in my living room. Like toxic waste, I can't seem to get rid of it.

So, yes, it's time to downsize.

We visit open houses and are either enchanted or perplexed by other people's homes. Why does every single home smell like Martha Stewart is baking cookies? Hey, and that's not a lake, that's a smelly retention pond. These trips make us consider the pros and cons of our own home. Why did we decorate our downstairs half-bath like a French whorehouse? Not that I've ever been in a French whorehouse, but I read.

Then we worry: Will our house ever sell? The gigantic elephant in the room is not the potential sale, but what to do with what we've accumulated from a marriage of 30-plus years. "Get rid of everything personal," the realtor advises. "Buyers want to see the house, not your life's story."

She's right. What is sad but becoming very apparent is: No one wants our stuff. Our son—the one we imagined would long for and quickly snap up our precious one-of-a-kind heirlooms—lives in a studio apartment in a large East Coast city.

He says he really can't squeeze my great-grandmother's Victrola record player on the plane in his carry-on bag, advising me to try Ebay, or failing that, to put the Victrola at the curb with a "Free" sign on it. And dragging that humongous breakfront onto the Metro Red Line during rush hour, would be kind of a bear. He suggested it might be good for firewood.

What were we thinking? Why do I keep a 12-inch inflatable plastic shark? I gave "Mee-ster Feesh," with his Sharpie-drawn moustache, to my future husband in college. Am I just clinging to him because he transports me to a younger, less-cluttered time? And really, who needs three 1920s mantle clocks that don't work? Then there's the champagne bottle from our honeymoon, an Elvis prayer candle, a collection of typewriters, including a classic manual Olympic, and an avalanche of sweatshirts in multiple colors from places near and far (because I always forget to bring something warm).

As for long-playing albums, my house is awash with them. There's the entire Barry Manilow collection, The Carpenters, and yes, Captain and Tennille. And books are everywhere: *The Riverside* and *The Sylvan Barnett* works of Shakespeare. Art books from favorite exhibitions and museum trips. Husband's fiction, my non-fiction.

We also have a collection of sepia-toned pictures—dust-catchers behind glass—on mantles, on counters, in dark-lined photo boxes and albums. Six Hummels from Germany are stuffed carelessly in discarded clothes after that visit with Great Aunt Zoe in Denver. After all this time, I guess the least I can do is release them.

Years ago, I used to fantasize about having the perfect dream home with every knick-knack telling its own enchanting story. These days, I dream of renting a large dumpster and tossing the whole lot out the window into the trash.

The truth is downsizing is not easy and punctuated with emotion and memories. Stuff is not love, but some stuff embodies love. How can I toss out a framed watercolor of *The Cat in the Hat* my son painted in kindergarten? What about my 1984 wedding dress? Then high fashion, the dress could be a Facebook meme today, warning brides, "What not to wear."

Still, I've come to the conclusion my vision of a sleek, modern, uncluttered, home is really not what homes are all about. A home is not its contents. A home is how those contents create a bond among those who share the space.

So after careful consideration, my husband and I will make peace with what stays and what goes. Instead of a massive bonfire, we'll sort through the relics of our lives well lived.

And probably keep most of it.

And wherever we wind up, we'll be fortunate to have a home filled with love and art, books and memories. And a plastic shark. One more thing— Did I mention I'm giving away a fantastic piano? It's a beautiful antique. It'd look lovely in your home.

Menopausal Maniacs in Mexico

by Janie Emaus

I'm bumping down the beach on a four-wheel quad. My dimpled butt is getting a workout of a lifetime. The wind whips my hair off my face, blowing it into dreadlocks, which I know will take at least fifteen minutes of rinsing and ten dollars' worth of conditioning for re-entry back to civilization. Sand gets into my eyes and nostrils. At some point, I'll need to rinse out those important body parts. But at this moment, I'm having too much fun to worry about it.

The sky is a dark blanket filled with hundreds of shiny pinpricks, as if heaven is looking down on us.

In front of me, seven ladies are zooming along

the sand. One by one they raise their hands in the air and sing.

"*Ai yi yi yi yi.*" Our voices carry down the beach and through the town.

It's a perfect evening in Baja, Mexico. It's freedom. No cell phones. No beeping and zinging. No to-do lists. No worries.

It's a birthday celebration like none other I've ever experienced. And I've lived through quite a lot.

From the picture I've painted you're probably assuming we are celebrating turning thirty or perhaps forty. After all, we are indulging in an activity associated with the young.

And you're partially right. Half the group are women turning thirty, the other half of the group, of which I am a proud member, are turning sixty.

Yes, we are entering our sixth decade with gusto. And why not? The last time I checked with a travel guide, being young and fit wasn't a prerequisite for acting wild and crazy at a beach. And after so many years on this planet, women of our age know how to put the Z in crazee!

Now of course, we "mature" señoras are celebrating a bit differently from our younger señoritas. We stay up much later, trying to remember what we learned in astronomy. We have enough trouble remembering the names of simple household items, so naming the constellations takes a great deal of concentration.

We get up with the sunrise, sipping coffee as the sun pops up like a big orange ball over the horizon. We clap with joy each morning, as if we hadn't expected it to appear.

We eat everything placed in front of us. If it's not moving, that is. We drink more. We share secrets. We flirt without restraint and expectations.

Why? Because with age comes wisdom. And a certain kind of freedom that lets you act without second-guessing yourself.

It also brings a few other changes, especially when it comes to packing.

Whereas the thirty-year-olds brought moisturizers, body oils, and SPF 15 sunscreen, we older ladies packed anti-aging face creams, puffy eye reduction oils, and SPF 500 sunblocks. And then after slathering on gobs of sun protector, we stretch out on lounges in the shade. Gone are the days of following the sun across the sky.

The younger girls brought birth control pills and vitamins. We wouldn't be caught dead without our hormone pills, calcium, antacids, high-blood-pressure meds, fish oil, and other memory-enhancing drugs.

The young women filled their suitcases with flowered sundresses, fancy sandals, and even high heels. We brought comfortable walking shoes, sweat pants, and tank tops.

Each thirty-year-old woman has several brightly colored bikinis. My friends and I all have one-piece suits with wraps. When we walk around in public, these cover our jiggling thighs and flappy arms.

The señoritas brought manicure sets, complete with nail buffers, cuticle softeners, and various polishes. We señoras made sure to have scrub brushes to get the dirt out of our fingernails after a long night of quad riding on the beach.

I've noticed we not only pack differently, we also carry different baggage with us. We señoras, thankfully, have developed a mindset that allows us to let that baggage go.

So, in the evening, while the young girls hover around their computers, posting the day's activities on social media and Skyping with their friends back home, we older ladies sit on the deck, sipping Margaritas and looking up at the sky. We know there will be plenty of time later to look at our photos and relive the trip. For now, we're going to live the trip. We're going to live in the moment.

The young girls feel the need to stay in touch with "real" life, sharing their every move. We señoras have checked out of "reality" for this week and checked into Paradise.

In the morning, we'll be riding again. Menopausal women with hot flashes taking the town by storm.

We know the local fisherman, the beach vendors, the Mariachi singers, and especially the bartenders. They know us, not as "older ladies" but as "That Crazy Quad Gang."

In thirty years when the young girls turn sixty, I hope I can be here to celebrate with them. I may be a bit slower at ninety. But I'll still be moving.

After all, age is just a state of mind. Of course, it helps to have a body that holds up. But there's nothing like driving a quad, at night, on the beach to keep your mind and body young.

As we señoras say: "*Ai yi yi yi yi.*"

"If I had my life to live over again, I would have eaten less cottage cheese and more ice cream."

—ERMA BOMBECK

Losing It
by Cindy Eastman

I'm dieting. Again. Both my husband and I are, but I'm the expert. He's a novice because he grew up thin and lanky, never bothered by the number of calories in a mug of beer or a bowl of ice cream.

It's aging that has him keeping an eye on his caloric intake. Otherwise, he'd be scarfing down pasta by the box, unregulated by those pesky portion sizes or cumbersome calorie counts. I, however, have been dieting since I was two. Adolescence was not my friend. And even during my first pregnancy, my doctor put me on a meal plan with a measly 1,800 calories a day. For me, there would be no eating for two; no Snickers bars that I imagined would be my daily snack.

Dieting has been a way of life for me. I've been on the Drinking Man's diet, the Eat-Right-for-Your-Type diet, and the Ice Cream diet, to name a few. I've been a Weight Watcher and a Carb Counter. I have friends who declared—after their babies were born—that they were going to "get back to when they were thinner." I had no such declaration; I was never thinner. One friend insisted she dropped a penny on her newly taut stomach—like twenty minutes after delivery—and it literally bounced off, like an Olympic gymnast. If I had done the same thing, my penny would have disappeared into the depths, never to be seen again.

Enter my helpful husband. Ever the trailblazing techie, he ran into the living room one day looking like the cat who ate the canary.

"I've got to show you something," he said excitedly. I thought he bought me a present, so I bit.

"So, what is it?" I asked coyly, thinking, *A romantic weekend? Tickets to Italy?*

"It's an app," he said. "You just download it on your phone and it keeps track of all the food you eat each day." I tried to contain my excitement.

"Wow, really? What fun," I said, mentally unpacking my suitcase.

"No, really, it's easy," he said, and then he went on—and on—and on—showing me how you can look up practically anything you eat, because the app is connected to an online database containing thousands of foods. No more fudging on calories or fat content. It's all right there. Oh joy.

"I can't wait to start," I fibbed. I slid my phone screen over to Sudoku and ignored him.

But later, when my husband wasn't around, I went ahead and downloaded the app, cheerfully called "My Fitness Pal," and entered my information. (Obviously, I lied about my current weight. That's none of my new pal's business.) After the data was calculated, I was "given" 1,200 calories a day. Total—not for each meal. I went over by 1,500 calories the first day. Not a great start. But as the weeks went by, I was able to stay within my limit and not feel like a starving Tom Hanks in the movie *Castaway*.

After a couple of months of this merriment, I made a startling discovery: I had been eating lots more food than I ever imagined. It's very easy to eyeball a slice of pizza and decide that, yeah, it's probably about six ounces, or whatever the recommended dosage is, when it really wasn't. However, when the app showed me the real calorie intake of my meals for the day, I was totally shocked. It proved that I had been eating three times the amount I should have been—all the while considering myself "on a diet."

Age may grind my metabolism practically down to a halt. But, I'm still me—a twenty-pounds-over-ideal-weight me. Even if I keep track of every little morsel, my belly will never be a trampoline for errant pennies. Blue jeans with a non-elastic waistband may be a thing of the past. And I'll always crave peanut-butter-and-potato-chip sandwiches. So, perhaps, I'll just have to accept that.

Besides a slower metabolism, with age, comes wisdom. And I think what I've learned from this experience is that dieting doesn't work for me. Because when I look back, most of my extra pounds are the result of incomparable three-hour meals of homemade cavatelli, red wine, and creamy pastries in Italy and family vacations in Maine, complete with buttery lobsters and blueberry pancakes. I equate those pounds to fond memories of the best times in my life. And I don't want to "diet" those happy times away.

Of course, paying attention to the food I put in my body is just plain healthy. And I plan to be more mindful of that. But I don't want to feel that my self-worth is dependent on whether I can or can't stay on a diet. It's a losing battle. I've come to the conclusion that "dieting" seems to trigger my inner saboteur. And she always wins. Somehow she can always talk me into indulging in a scoop of vanilla ice cream atop a warm chocolate brownie. So I won't give her the chance. There will be no more dieting for me.

Wait until I tell my husband.

"Come on, Inner Peace. I don't have all day."

—SACHIN GARG

Sweating Bullets: Hot Yoga and My Search for Inner Peace

by Pamela Wright

I greeted the New Year with a vow to get my act together. The holiday season had left me depressed and bloated. Perhaps it was the advent of my 45th birthday just before Christmas, or the two weeks of over-indulgence in carbs and self-pity. I was in serious danger of crossing the line into zaftig, or even worse, being described as "real pretty in the face." So I began with a recommitment to physical fitness.

Google revealed an interesting prospect: a hot yoga studio near my home in Atlanta. I knew several yoga devotees—centered, peaceful women who extolled the virtues of meditative breathing and properly aligned chakras. And they could wear skinny jeans with their shirts tucked in above their remarkably perky asses.

I arrived early for the Sunday morning session, anticipating a spandex-swaddled Nirvana. A petite woman introduced herself as the instructor and suggested my goal should be to simply remain in the room for the entire class. I found that curious, but dismissed it as yoga-speak.

After I signed an extensive liability waiver, the instructor pointed me toward the studio. As I turned away, she added, "Oh, and we lock the door after class starts."

They lock the door? I debated whether I should point out this constituted unlawful restraint, or possibly even kidnapping.

The instructor entered the steamy studio and took her place before the mirrored front wall. "It seems we have quite a few first-timers this morning, so the class may run a little long," she announced with a hint of exasperation. "I'll have to talk you through all 26 poses in more detail than usual."

Twenty-six poses? Sweat was already rolling down every surface of my body.

As she directed us into the Pranayama pose, I noticed the instructor didn't participate. She just barked instructions like a drill sergeant ordering a line of recruits. I laced my hands beneath my chin and raised my elbows above my ears. A guttural din rose around me as we were instructed to open our jaws and produce a hissing, gurgling noise from deep within our tracheas. I tried to follow along, but quickly choked on saliva. The instructor warned we might become dizzy or feel a pinch in our shoulder.

Aren't those symptoms of a heart attack?

The Eagle pose involved intertwining the forearms and hands, and coiling the legs together like stripes on a candy cane, all while balancing on one foot. My sweaty hands disentangled with such force that my knuckles smacked me in the face and I pitched over into the formidably muscled woman beside me.

"Sorry," I whispered.

"No talking during class!" the instructor bellowed.

I snapped to attention and struggled to execute the poses, all of which defied basic principles of human anatomy. They also defied the elastic in my yoga pants. With every stance, I felt the waistband creep down my hips, lower and lower. I feared the next move would send my pants rolling south, allowing the holiday-softened flesh within to erupt like a busted can of biscuits.

The temperature rose with each interminable minute. I was panting like a dog, but felt encouraged when I saw others were also experiencing difficulty. It began quietly, with the faintest *"heeee-ushhh-heeee-ushhhh"* emanating from the far corners of the room. It soon sounded like I was trapped inside the world's largest iron lung.

We were on our stomachs, with limbs stretched upward behind us. As I attempted to grasp my sweat-slicked ankles, the woman beside me intoned *"Oooh-EEEE-oooh-EEEE"* from between her bared teeth, like some kind of New Age hog caller. A middle-aged man behind her seemed to be speaking in tongues, crying, *"AH-yee-oma-nama-OH."* It all melded into cacophony more hellish than the Metallica concert I attended in 1987 while high on peach schnapps and Lebanese hash.

Later, we were instructed to reach through and behind the legs until our heads were nearly up our own behinds. My head only made it to about knee level. I watched sweat stains creep southward from my crotch and comingle into a pattern reminiscent of a Rorschach ink blot. I hung there, trying to decide if it looked more like a flock of sheep or Teddy Roosevelt on horseback, until I began to lose consciousness. I returned to a standing position, gasping as if in the throes of childbirth.

Just as I began to consider crawling beneath my mat to await the sweet relief of asphyxia, the instructor announced the class was over. She recommended we lie quietly for another fifteen to twenty minutes. I considered that advice for about a millisecond before leaping up like LeBron James and spanning the forty-odd feet between myself and the door in one step. The locked door didn't discourage me one bit; I was prepared to hurl myself against it, like a TV cop, until it broke free from its hinges or my shoulder broke free from my body.

My bravado would never be tested. The door sprang open at the lightest touch, sending me sprawling onto the floor on the other side. I laid there on the cool tiles as the other students filed out. The instructor was the last to exit, and I rose up on my elbows as she passed.

"Didn't you say y'all lock the door once class starts?" I asked.

She stopped and stood over me with her hands on her hips.

"Yes," she said. "We lock the *front* door. We've had some thefts recently."

She knitted her eyebrows. "You didn't think I meant we locked you in there, did you? That would be illegal," she said and walked off.

However much I envied my yogi friends, this class was not for me. I knew the closest I would ever come to reaching Nirvana was digging out my old Kurt Cobain mix tapes. Although the morning had fallen short of my expectations, I remained undeterred in my search for an activity to lift both spirit and booty.

Maybe I'll try water aerobics next, I thought to myself. *My neighbor loves it, and she's in great shape. She doesn't look a day over 79.*

It's All in the Way You View Things

by Lorraine Ray

If there's one thing I strive to have more of in my life, it's a hefty dose of perspective. It helps me view the world to my advantage. The late actress, Shelley Winters, had the right idea. "I'm not overweight," she said wisely. "I'm just nine inches too short." Now, that's perspective.

I remember a classic *Twilight Zone* episode, "Eye of the Beholder," depicting a critically disfigured woman undergoing her eleventh surgery to try to look "normal." After the medical team breaks the news that the surgery failed, the woman's bandages are removed, and we see a stunning, classic beauty surrounded by a grotesque, monstrous-looking medical team. They were the norm, the desirables; she was the ugly outcast. It was scary because of one thing: perspective.

Yes, friends, it's all in the way you view things. We're not old and dowdy. We are antique treasures. We're "flabby" chic, chronologically enhanced, and oozing with character and charm. If furniture, tchotchkes, and fine wine are more valuable when they age, why aren't people? And particularly women? Why is "distressed" furniture charming, but a weather-worn woman a hag? Why isn't old age worshipped instead of youth? Why don't those sweet young things of 20 and 30 wish they looked like us? Instead, we're knocking ourselves out trying to look like them. Maybe we have the wrong point of view?

But what if the vista changed? What if wrinkles were in and smooth skin were to be avoided at all costs? We'd probably be hearing more conversations like this:

WOMAN 1: How do you do it? You've completely lost the youthful look you once had. In fact, you've aged much more than I have. What's your secret? I mean, I'm really jealous. Have you had work done?

WOMAN 2: Well, it all started just before my class reunion. I was, like, totally disgusted with my appearance. I felt pitifully vibrant and rosy.

Can you believe my complexion was even dewy? Gag. I looked way too young for my age, quite one-dimensional, with no sign of character. I knew I needed to act quickly; I wanted to look at least ten years older for the reunion. I wanted to see the green of envy in my peers' eyes. And, why not? After all, I'm worth it. And there are things a woman can do.

WOMAN 1: Absolutely. I'm with you. So, did you have work done?

WOMAN 2: It depends how you define "work." I was hoping to show off a few wrinkles, some marionette lines, a foreshadowing of jowls. But, everything was tight—I couldn't find a fold or sag anywhere. I did what I could to accelerate the aging process. Sat out in the sun; went to tanning salons, stayed up late. But I still looked like my senior class picture. I asked my doctor if surgery could make me look like Granny Clampett on *The Beverly Hillbillies*. But, he admitted, even with surgery, he could never make me look that glamorous.

WOMAN 1: Go on, go on. You must have done something.

WOMAN 2: Well, I got wind of a promising new line of pro-aging products called "Parched Sahara." So I bought out the store and slathered them on every night, religiously. I focused on my teeth, next—just like they do on television makeover shows. I faithfully applied Frest Yellow-Strips, and that took the "sparkly white" away. Then, I went to a cosmetic dentist who completed my look with some enhanced crookedness. I couldn't wait for my classmates with boring Chiclet smiles to see me.

WOMAN 1: I'm envious. Your teeth are amazing—dingy, overcrowded, perfect.

WOMAN 2: That was just the beginning. I also committed myself to a strict routine of non-exercise. My firm arms and flat abs were a dead giveaway: I'd let myself go, for sure. Okay, so I occasionally caved in to some lazy habits of aerobics and resistance training. But I caught myself and went back to the couch, binge watching Netflix and munching chips, guzzling soda, and chomping chocolate-covered peanuts.

WOMAN 1: Wow, but it was all worth it. Look at you. You've gotten back that true post-menopausal flab. In fact, you've gone up a couple of dress sizes, haven't you? And look at me. I'm a mess. I look like I've been running marathons. I can't seem to find the willpower to slow down and stop binging on veggies. Did you do anything else?

WOMAN 2: Well, you know I didn't have surgery. But I discovered a great makeup line that would help me achieve significant results anyway. I found some awesome wrinkle revealers for lines, and low lighters for darkness, shadows, and tiredness. My hair was another easy fix. I used a good toner in steely gray with just a hint of violet for that authentic blue-hair glow that everyone wants.

WOMAN 1: Your hair looks fantastic. I'm so sick of this shiny, voluminous mess. You look absolutely amazing, so old and distinguished. You'll probably turn 70 and look 90. If anyone can do it, you can.

Biddies, bubbies, and boomers, the fault is not in us—nor in our stars. It's in our perspective. It's like believing we're fat when we're only short. It's like feeling we're frumpy when we're actually sophisticated. It's like thinking we're old hags when we're really fairy tale godmothers.

My advice? Change the way we view ourselves. Change our outlook. We are vintage vixens, dinged-up darlings, dimpled doyens. We are valuable, to be sought after and coveted. We are what every young woman should hope to grow up to be. So, my friends, remember it's all in the way we look at things. And from my vantage point, it's all good.

"Time spent with cats is never wasted."

—SIGMUND FREUD

Hi, I'm Allia and I'm Cat Codependent
by Allia Zobel Nolan

I consider myself a forceful woman—not given to many crutches. No night light keeps vigil while I sleep. Spiders don't make me squeamish. I know where the oil goes in my car. I am a woman of a certain age, but so far, that has never held me back. Still, I do have this one overwhelming Achilles heel (and it's not from my Christian Louboutins). It's because of my cats. I love them too much.

So, okay, I admit it: I'm cat codependent. It's an addiction I've struggled with all my life.

But happily, these days, I'm not alone. Women (and men) everywhere have caught on to what I've known for years: There's no getting "enough" of cats, which is why an ailurophile like myself will spend hours on Facebook and YouTube pawing over cat videos. That is, when I'm not trolling the Net for cat clothing, jewelry, tattoos, or coupons for the latest cat café. Why I've even considered plastic surgery to look more like my cat.

Still, it wasn't always like this. In the days before Grumpy Cat and Lil Bub, people thought I was a joke, the infamous cat lady gone over the edge.

"Did you notice her upper lip?" one of my business associates cackled. "She looks like she's sprouting whiskers."

"Yeah, and her briefcase stinks of salmon," another answered. "It's horribly unprofessional."

"What about those earrings?" yet another associate chimed in. "She makes them from her cats' fur. Disgusting."

Yet what did those naysayers know? Back then, the general populace thought a cat was, well, just a cat. They had no idea. It's only now that cats are getting the respect they deserve. It's only recently that people have come to see them as the loyal, loving, entertaining creatures they are. It's only today that the cat reclaims the honored place she had back when pharaohs wore snakes on their heads and people rode to work in chariots.

And talk about being in synch.

I've never met any human that could ever

match my cats. Oh, my husband comes close. But even he has his limitations. In all the years I've known him, he's never once run down the stairs and rubbed against my legs the minute I walk in. Then, too, when I'm in the tub, he doesn't sit quietly alongside like the cats, grooming himself. And if I fall asleep on the couch after a hard day's work, you won't catch him perched on my stomach, purring and kneading me, like they do. Oh sure, he has his attributes. It's just that my cats are infinitely more "simpatico."

Even in this age of the cat, though, some people still snicker that I go overboard. They don't realize I'm in recovery, and things take time. However, I am getting better. Litter by litter.

Why only last week, I bought scoopable on sale instead of the designer-brand litter I've imported in the past. I saved two bucks, but I felt like a cad. True to their self-sacrificing nature, the little darlings took it on the chin. They only did their business twice on the rug.

Truth is I have had to cut back in other ways, too. And it almost broke my heart. It isn't easy explaining to fur children who're used to having the air conditioning and *Animal Planet* on all day that they have to sweat and look out the window.

But I have put my foot down. I no longer open up tin after tin of cat food to find one they like.

I've set a limit of nine. I've also canceled the cats' animal enrichment classes with their mind-body counselor, Ulma.

What's more, no cats eat from our plates anymore. I bought them their own bone china. And I don't jump up each time they want to leave the room. All the doors, including the powder room, now have cat flaps.

So I'm making some progress. And the fact is, with so many other women (and men) coming out of the bag about their cat codependency these days, I feel much better. I don't feel so alone...so ostracized.

But for now, I'll just finish massaging Nolan Nolan's temples. He gets those awful sinus headaches when he stays out all night. Then, maybe I'll surprise the kitties with a real treat.

I mean how hard can it be to give a cat a French manicure?

"Yes, I'm 124 years old.
My secret: Wine, laughter and a massage."

—PINTEREST

Feeling Kneady
by Alice Muschany

By the time the Big Six-0 hit, menopause netted me my fair share of gray hairs along with more than a few extra pounds, and hot flashes so intense, global warming may well be my fault.

Family and friends surprised me on the day with a birthday party. Downing a few glasses of Chardonnay gave me the courage to open gifts that included Depends, Clairol Nice 'n Easy hair color, Pond's moisturizer, and Geritol. In addition to gag gifts, girlfriends gave me a certificate for a full-body massage. A massage at my age? There's a first time for everything.

A few weeks later, when yard work left me with sore muscles and a stiff back, I remembered the certificate and reluctantly scheduled an appointment. Just the thought of some young hunk glimpsing my love handles had me sweating profusely. Then again, the embarrassment might be worth it if he managed to get the kinks out of my aching body.

I thumbed through the salon's brochures, while I nervously waited my turn. One advertisement offered a special on hot-stone massage. *No thanks,* I thought to myself. *My mother taught me not to play with fire.*

My heart pounded when the receptionist called my name and motioned for me to follow. She ushered me into a room where she instructed me to undress as much as I felt comfortable with.

Is taking off nothing enough? I wondered. Beads of perspiration gathered on my mustache as I searched the room for hidden cameras. When I couldn't find them (but I knew they were there), I finally ditched most of my clothes and cowered beneath the sheet on the massage table, praying the dimly lit room was dark enough to hide my cellulite.

The sheet wrinkle I reached down to smooth turned out to be my own Pillsbury Dough-girl-stomach, most likely that cinnamon roll I had for breakfast. Make that two cinnamon rolls. Still, I'm sure there aren't too many women my age with 24-inch waists like talk-show host Kelly Ripa.

Even so, lying on the table, I started to stress.

That ignited my hot flashes and I could feel the flimsy white cover sticking to my body. But after a while, the eucalyptus aroma and relaxed music caused my eyelids to grow heavy—until the three cups of coffee I'd drunk earlier along with the sound of the flowing waterfall—assaulted my bladder.

Crossing my legs, I tried distracting myself. It didn't work. I worried one sneeze and it would be all over—literally.

I was afraid a Brad Pitt look-alike would walk in any minute and get a peek at my granny panties. So I was relieved when a tall, large-boned woman opened the door. She asked, in a heavy German accent, how I liked my massage.

Since I really didn't know, I replied, "I like it hard."

The woman didn't tell me her name. But if I had to guess, it would have been Helga. *Hope Helga doesn't think me a bad girl*, I thought.

"Helga" went straight to work. She grabbed my calf and proceeded to knead my muscle like my grandmother used to pound the dough for homemade bread. Then she began deep-massaging the small of my back with a vengeance. I wondered if she played linebacker for some football team on the side.

As the brute-force pummeling continued, I flinched and yelped like a kicked dog, hoping for a little mercy. Helga must have misunderstood because she pressed even harder. *Didn't the brochure promise a gentle Swedish massage?*

Next, this moose, I mean, this masseuse, focused on my shoulders and slowly made her way up to my neck.

Then she massaged my scalp. Soft moans escaped my lips—until she reached down and yanked my hair like a contestant in the Women's World Wide Wrestling Federation. My first instinct was to retaliate by grabbing hers, but she wore it cropped short. Besides, the last time I pulled anyone's hair was back in kindergarten.

Absurdly ticklish, my legs shot out when she touched my feet. Before long, my giggles were silenced. The best way to describe the foot massage was "*Ahhhhh.*" A girl could get used to this.

All too soon Helga barked, "Roll over."

In my dream state, I leisurely slipped onto my back, but not before giving her an eyeful of flesh when the sheet tangled underneath me. Her thumb tugged none too gently below my eye, and I worried she'd aggravate the wrinkles those outrageously expensive creams were supposed to erase. She rubbed my cheeks until I was sure they were bright red. It was painful in a good way.

Next, her fingers began to gently caress my face. OMG! She must have grown another hand. When she softly stroked my temples, I purred. My contented sighs increased as her feathery touch continued to perform magic. The brochure lived up to its promise after all. An almost-spiritual peace overtook me and I wondered: *Did I just die and go to heaven?*

No sooner had I slipped into a blissful state, then Helga broke off. My subconscious heard, "Wir ar finished," but my body whispered, "Nein, nein. Please don't stop."

The sound of the slamming door brought me out of my trance. In my stress-free state, I decided not to wait for another birthday that ends in zero for my next massage. Turns out it's something I definitely "knead."

Who knows? I might even ask for Helga.

Color Me Happy
by Amy Hartl Sherman

Skin is the largest organ of the human body. Mine is getting larger by the minute. Failing elasticity is giving way to a saggy, crepey, wrinkly epidermal mess. My solution? Tattoos.

In a modern-day twist of things, I'm publishing my memoir in picture form, on the best canvas ever: my body. While some will spend money to have their skin cut, pulled, and tightened as the years go by, I'll use my skin as my palette. Instead of making it more compact and condensed, I'll make it more colorful and personal. Instead of crying over the changes I see, I'll paint in the empty space with images and words that will be serve as my very own illustrated history.

Batwings, those dangling pieces of fat flapping from our underarms, make the perfect location for animated ink—maybe a native girl who can dance the hula whenever I wave goodbye to friends. Or perhaps I'll get an ocean scene with actual waves slapping me in the face as I wiggle the hanging flesh for effect. I mean, why not celebrate my skin as I get older, instead of criticizing it?

I remember my first tattoo. It was a fortieth birthday present to myself. That was 22 years ago. Back then, I was worried about what impression having a tattoo would leave on some small-minded people. Plus, I had little kids and I didn't want to embarrass them in front of their friends. So I played it safe. I got a tulip on my lower abdomen. This way, when I took my kids to the school pool, my swimsuit would cover it. No need to have the pool janitor (the one plastered with tatts) thinking I was a kindred spirit—a reason to start up a conversation.

Even my then-six-year-old son cautioned me to choose a tatt very carefully. He was concerned about the permanence. I love him for that. Still, tulips are my favorite flower, so I felt pretty sure there would be no regrets.

Over a decade later, in my sixties, I felt it was past time to hit a parlor again. I'd been looking for ideas when an artist I admired came to Chicago and we hooked up through emails. Because I had worked as a flight attendant for American Airlines, I figured that would make a great tatt. I was right as this tattooer did an awesome job. And now I had added a youthful image from a very happy time to my repertoire. It was (is) perfect.

That was the beginning of my idea for a tattoo memoir. Within months, I added two more meaningful chapters. One was a quill since I write. It doubles as a buddy tatt because a friend had the same image done at the same time on her neck. That is a memory worth every penny and needle prick.

The next tattoo was a spontaneous jump. The day a certain male Republican Senator asked a certain female Democratic Senator to stop reading a letter from a certain wife of a slain Civil Rights Giant, I knew I'd found the quote I'd been hungering for: "Nevertheless, she persisted." Those three words sum up women's history, as well as my own. And now that I have them close by, I can look to them when I need a powerful reminder to persevere.

I have others tattoos in mind, but I'm waiting to find the right artist. That's an important part of the process. I won't wait long, though. At 62, I feel I'm running out of time. See, I want to look at my skin, now, with wonder and awe, not shock and disappointment. And for me, at least, this is the way to do that. Instead of just holding my organs and bones in place (which I'm not knocking, mind you), I've found an exciting new purpose for my skin: It's coloring my life.

Though I'm not sure where it will go, I know I'll be adding a flying pig. This will be my reminder of the days I was in a Chicago improv group called "Pigwings." I also want to add the initials of my family, which just so happen to be "A,B,C,D." When it comes to tattoos, deciding what to have inked is half the fun.

I compare getting a tatt to childbirth. It's plenty painful. It takes some tending afterwards. But it's worth every bloody minute. Like childbirth, you can talk through the process, and like childbirth, you can't wait until it's over. Then, like you do with a new baby, you can't stop looking at it. What's more, despite the labor pains of pounding needle into flesh, you can't wait to get your next one.

As far as I can see, the only drawback to a tatt is that it prevents me from going on any major crime sprees. Tatts are easy identifiers. So I guess if I ever fantasized shoplifting at Tiffany or stealing a flavored water from the local 7-Eleven, I can forget about that.

Sill, my tatts will serve me well if I end up dead in a ditch somewhere with no I.D. If this happens, I won't be relegated to a cold slab at the morgue, with a toe tag marked "Identity Unknown." Lots of people will be able to confirm who I am based on my Facebook posts alone.

Because what's the point of getting a tattoo if you aren't going to share it on social media?

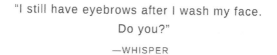

"I still have eyebrows after I wash my face.
Do you?"

—WHISPER

Hanging on by a Thread

by Sharon Gerger

My bank statement arrived today. It doesn't usually scare me. I mean, I work at the bank that mails the statement. So I pretty much know what's happening in my pathetic little account on a daily basis.

My husband, however, never looks at it. Today, though, he was bored. So he tore open the envelope. And, because he was really bored, he added up what I'd spent on personal care appointments and products, or as he referred to them, "crap."

I ripped the statement from his grubby little paws and proceeded to figure out the amounts he spent at area fishing-gear stores. And he won, that is, he lost, as it appeared I outspent him. In any event, he skulked away.

Left alone, I checked the numbers and was horrified to see how much I'd actually forked out on haircuts, highlights, cosmetics, fancy shampoos, conditioners, gels and mousses, facials, manicures and pedicures, all in an effort to make myself look halfway decent in public. Worse than that, I was reminded of a recent expenditure that I, frankly, would pay anything to forget.

I was having my nails done at a local salon when I noticed a sign that read: "Eyebrow Threading Special—Today Only—$8.00." Now I usually had a hot wax treatment to keep my superfluous eyebrows in line. This consisted of having wax applied, and then once it cooled, having it ripped off, along with the offensive brow hairs. It hurts...a lot.

I looked at the sign again. Threading. The word sounded so peaceful and calm. I remembered my sister, Kim, telling me she has her eyebrows threaded and it doesn't really hurt. "It's just a little uncomfortable," she explained once. I tend to forget that Kim's an ICU nurse who has told patients that poking a tube through the flesh between their ribs to re-inflate a collapsed lung might be "a little uncomfortable." But, what the heck.

I asked and was thrilled when the salon

owner said it was possible to have my eyebrows done immediately. She moved me to a little table across from a lady who told me she'd be happy to help me. She didn't look happy, but then, she didn't look like she would harm me either.

After she examined my eyebrows, she unwound about eight yards of thread. (It'd been a while since I'd had my brows done.) Then she leaned in closer, ran her hand up and down the side of my face, and reported that I had a very hairy face, very hairy, very long hair. She added that my very hairy face looked very bad. It made me look very old.

"I can thread whole face. Only $38," she said, with a promise that I'd appear much younger. Well, how could I say no, now that I'd been told I was basically an aging Sasquatch?

She did the brows first. She somehow wrapped the thread around several dozen hairs at the same time and then flicked it causing dozens of hairs to rip from deep within my flesh. She repeated this a few times until both brows met her satisfaction. Meantime, I struggled not to slump to the floor in a dead faint.

I figured the worst was over. I mean the brow area is sensitive, right? The sides of my face and chin, well, how much could that hurt?

The pain was beyond anything I ever imagined and I've given birth to a ten-pound baby! It took the lady thirty minutes to tear all the extraneous hair from my face, including a brief break so I could mop up tears after she assaulted my upper lip. When she was done, she looked at me admiringly, and asked, "How old are you?"

I told her I was sixty. She smiled triumphantly and said I looked only fifty-six. Fifty-six? A half-hour of agony bought me just four years?

As I staggered away from her little torture station, I braved a peek in the mirror. The face of someone who'd be beaten and left in an alley looked back at me.

I had mascara halfway down my cheeks from crying, and bright-red splotches, some still oozing blood, in what was left of my skin. I also had dabs of white chalk that the lady had used on my face, presumably to keep the hairs from matting in my tears. I wondered if she'd gotten the chalk from the police after they'd outlined the body of her last victim.

I stopped staring and cleaned myself up as best I could, considering how weak I was, what with the blood loss and all. Then I went to the cashier and actually paid for what they had done to me. The woman took my money and informed me that I was to come back in three weeks to have the whole procedure repeated again.

This was necessary, she said, if I wanted to continue to look very young.

I thought to myself, *I think I'll risk it.* The worst that can happen is that I will look my age—a little hairier, perhaps. But I can live with that.

When I got home, I told my husband he's welcome to spend what I save on threading for his fishing lures.

Loving the Skin I'm In

by Sherri Kuhn

I see you sizing me up in the grocery store, you sweet young thing. Your gaze wanders from my sensible shoes and comfy capris upward towards my time-weathered neck and dark-ringed eyes. I can almost hear you make a mental note to never, ever, get old. A smirk forms at the crinkly corners of my mouth as I watch you take stock of my obvious fashion fails and unimaginable lack of makeup.

You may not be able to place this feeling yet. But I'll give you a hint: it's green and mean, and some people call it a "monster." Envy.

Go ahead—let it sink in. You want to be just like me. You just don't know it yet. And one day, in the not-to-distant future, you should be so lucky.

I didn't get this way overnight, you know. Turning into a midlife goddess, completely relaxed in my body, takes time and dedication. It requires:

- willingness to forgo spinning class and the yoga studio for vanilla scones and an extra-large mocha
- guts to skip lipstick and mascara when grocery shopping or running errands
- strength to sacrifice the nail salon/spa facial/expensive tooth-whitening gel in favor of buying a college textbook for your kid
- courage to wear whatever you want, women-of-a-certain-age fashion rules be damned
- acceptance of reality and the peace of finally being comfortable in your own skin.

And this skin? It's the one I was born with. No dermatologic enhancements, surgery, or pricey potions here. Where you see wrinkles and age spots, I see time-tested battle armor.

After all, this skin has protected me through a childhood of scraped knees and countless bug bites; through the scalding sunburn I got from lying by the pool, covered in baby oil and iodine; through the stretch marks that accompanied being pregnant with two babies. I have been bruised, burned, and even broken—and this skin withstood the punishment.

Still, my skin is soft and supple. I'm squishy

when you hug me. And while my thighs and bottom may be somewhat thin, I've acquired a certain plumpness that descended in middle age—a cushion you might not notice when you eyeball me in the checkout line.

This padding started settling in sometime in my mid-40s. I admit, back then, I wasn't thrilled when the scale began to soar and my waistband pinched. But now? Bring it on. This coming-of-age cushion that surrounds me might not be youthful or sexy. But it has its benefits: it allows me to sit, painless, for hours chatting with an old friend, to binge-watch *Breaking Bad*, or to go on a long road trip comfortably.

And these wrinkles? Each and every one was earned—staying up late with a sick baby, crying over a loved one lost, or just laughing my head off at life's inanities. I know you want them. But they're mine. You'll earn your own in time.

I see you eyeing my hair. You probably pay big bucks every month for gorgeous streaks to accent your natural color, or maybe you blow a fortune to turn your hair bright red or blue.

My highlights are silver and shiny, quite possibly the color of angel's wings. They grow in neatly organized rows at my roots without fail, making their appearance every four to six weeks. They're little soldiers in the war that age is waging on my scalp. I bet you wish they were yours. Someday, young one.

So, I may not be a celebrity in the series *Scandal* or be featured on the cover of *People Style Watch*. But when I walk through my own front door? I'm a star. People fall at my feet begging—some for a home-cooked meal, or a few free loads of clean laundry, or my autograph as co-signer on an off-campus rental lease. I am one VIP as I glide effortlessly through my home tending to the masses and changing lives as I adjust my tiara.

My husband treats me like I'm a twenty-year-old version of Cindy Crawford. He looks past the spider veins, laugh lines, and floppy arms. So I soak up his attention and give it right back.

Unlike Nora Ephron, I don't feel bad(ly) about my neck. And my life's purpose doesn't depend on the clothes I wear or the flash of my whiter-than-white teeth. It goes deeper than that. The years have taught me to be thankful and satisfied with who I am and what I've become.

I'm proud of the skin I'm in. And it probably shows. So, in the end, perhaps I am a person to be envied. I hope someday, sweet young thing, you'll be envied, too.

Why Have Cod When You Could Have Lobster?

by Allia Zobel Nolan

Today's media is awash with features on rich and famous women who are into May-December romances. Shucks, I married a younger man and I'm neither. And that's the point.

Savvy glitterati have been on to the notion that younger is better for years. No one had to convince Madonna, Mariah, or Cameron Diaz. As for your average Jo(sephine), more and more, like moi, are beginning to see the light. In fact, most women reading this probably have a friend or acquaintance who's involved with a younger man— be it two months or ten years—and loving it.

Why have cod when you could have lobster? Why limit yourself because of someone else's (we don't even know whose) unwritten rule of thumb? Granted, some older woman-younger man relationships don't work out. But then, neither do some "age-appropriate" matches.

Bottom line is relationships are as different as the people in them, and you never know until you're involved. However, I firmly believe it's time women reprogram their ideas to accept that choosing a younger mate is an okay thing.

Men do it. That's right, the male of our species has been marrying and otherwise dallying with younger women since homo became erectus. I don't know exactly where the custom began. But, I'd bet my support hose, it was male-initiated. Probably some Neanderthal father trying to rake in a few animal hides by unloading his teenage daughter on the first Methuselah who showed any interest. All in her best interests, mind you, since older men usually had the stability and wherewithal to "take care of" the younger woman.

Today, most women can take care of themselves. And though (before I was wed) I wouldn't have looked askance at a relationship with a trillionaire who wanted me to quit work and shop non-stop just because he had a few miles on him, by the same token, I would not have passed up the same opportunity with a similar suitor because he was younger.

Oh, and don't be fooled into thinking there aren't enough men to go around. Statistics show that from ages 25 to 39, unmarried men outnumber women. Admittedly, as women mature (I hate the word "age"), we outnumber men. But that's simply because men tend to kick the bucket sooner. So considering the rise in life spans for females, it just makes good common sense to pick someone with less mileage, someone who won't wear out as fast.

What's in it for him? Plenty. For starters, there's the not-to-be-discounted psychobabble about men looking for a mother image. Everyone loves to be babied now and again and longing to be taken care of is not exclusive to females. Then, too, there's the age-old fascination, allure, and mystic of the older woman. To many a laddie, being with her is his fantasy come true.

Another plus: What he sees is more or less what he gets. We older women aren't prone to too many life changes. So if we haven't already gotten fat, lost our marbles, or maxed out our credit cards at this stage of the game, we're not as apt to. As my favorite younger man (my husband) so succinctly put it when I asked him what he sees in older women: "You never have to worry about how they'll turn out."

Today's older women don't stay home

crocheting doilies. We're more attractive, healthier, educated, confident, and interesting than ever before. What's more, we have smaller hair and bigger bank accounts. What's not to like?

I say if you've got eyes for a younger man, ignore the raised eyebrows and go for it. Don't let your insecurities trip you up. Don't constantly check yourself out in the mirror. You know what you look like, and he does, too. So give your younger man some credit. If he didn't like what he sees, he wouldn't be where he is—at your side.

You can sabotage yourself by playing the martyr, too. So don't. Don't put words in his mouth. And don't make assumptions he never would. He thinks you're the best thing since the microwave. So don't blow it.

And if you're worried about those long-legged, tight-bunned Lolitas out there ready to lure him away, chill. Yes, there are gorgeous young sirens skulking about. For the mature woman, this is an unpleasant fact of life—like roaches or dust balls. But it's a fact you're just going to have to get used to.

Remember, any man with working retinas will glance at an attractive girl. But that's true whether he's twenty-six or sixty. He's not making comparisons; he's just being human.

As for bosses who sneer, parents who clutch their hearts, and friends who confess concern for your welfare, when they see how happy you are, they'll get over it. As for strangers staring, maybe they are, or maybe it's your imagination. But why should you care anyway?

Finally, should people be crass enough to ask you what you see in a younger man, wink and tell them: he can thread a needle in under a minute, prefers bungee jumping to golf, and best of all, still believes in happily ever after.

> "Laughing is the best exercise;
> it's like running inside your mind."
>
> —ANONYMOUS

My Fitbit and I
by Sandy Lingo

My daughter knows my aversion to movement. Really, I am a pet rock. Except for brief runs (well, walks, to be honest) to the fridge and john, I could be a wax figure in Madame Tussaud's Museum. So it came as some surprise when my daughter sent her manatee-of-a-mother that fancy-pants pedometer that's so popular these days: a Fitbit.

When I got online to set up my Fitbit ("It takes literally three minutes," my daughter lied), I saw that mine was one of the basic models that costs $150. I can't believe my daughter bought such an expensive gift so totally wrong for me. But at least she didn't buy one of the more deluxe models that checks your heart rate and makes iced tea.

My Fitbit is in a serviceable black vinyl band. It tells the time and the date. It works like a pedometer, but oh-so-much more. In addition to counting steps, it determines how many miles I've walked, calories I've burned, and stairs I've climbed. These are all totally useless features for me. However, the good news is my Fitbit will also measure and assess the quality of my sleep. Now those are stats I can get into.

Because my daughter spent so much money on this thingie, I felt obligated to strap it on and begin the process. "It will change your life," my daughter said, and it has.

Wearing a Fitbit tells the world that, although I may look lumpy and saggy, I'm a woman who takes care of herself, a gal who makes the best of what she's got. A woman who most probably commits to daily flossing, meditation, and kegels. One who moves intentionally and with a certain amount of glee.

What's more, I hoard my steps like pieces of eight. I get in the shower with my Fitbit, then take it off and fling it on the counter so I don't miss a precious step. Imagine how horrified I was yesterday when I realized, after walking seven blocks to the post office, that I had left my Fitbit charging on my nightstand. I made my husband bring me my beloved gadget because there was no way I was going to waste steps that weren't counted. (He didn't mind because he was wearing *his* Fitbit.)

Then, too, losing my memory has become a good thing. I walk into a room and can't remember why I went there. I walk back to my recliner, and a commercial on TV reminds me that I need to put the laundry in the dryer. I head back to the laundry room, stopping on the way to water my philodendron. And then I return to my recliner where I remember I want to wear my white capris, which reminds me I need to get them out of the dryer, except they are still in the washer. Thanks to those white capris, and my bad memory, I've logged 489 steps.

When you know you have to walk anyway, it seems so much more enticing if you can do it in your bare feet and pjs. It turns out that the Fitbit doesn't care if you ever leave your house. You can cover a lot of miles pushing around a vacuum cleaner. You can climb a ladder to dust the top of your refrigerator or wash the windows. You can earn the Good Housekeeping Seal while reaching your Fitbit goal.

A bonus of my Fitbit is that it allows "two-for-one." This means if you sweat on an elliptical or treadmill, you accumulate steps even if you've been on, well, a treadmill. So when I go for my physical, I can tell the doctor, "I walked 10,000 steps today and did a half-hour aerobic exercise," without ever having to confess the overlap.

Sometimes to fill my Fitbit quota, I really need to get creative. It's 8:30 p.m., and I've only walked 8,962 steps. What to do? The Heart Association says I need to walk 10,000 steps a day. So I decided to concentrate more on my husband's needs.

"Would you like some wine?" I ask him, carefully offering to fetch only one thing. The trip to the wine cellar (which is located conveniently in the bottom kitchen cabinet next to the Triscuits) bumps me up to almost 9,000 steps.

"How about a cookie?" I ask.

"Oh, you'll need a napkin with that," I coo.

"May I refresh your glass?" I offer.

My unsuspectingly husband is so taken by this sudden attention, that he takes my hand and walks me to the bedroom. I check my Fitbit . . . 9,882.

"Yes!" I yell. My husband thinks I mean something else.

People say that sexual activity will impact your Fitbit stats. I'm not sure how, though. If you have the deluxe model, it'd register a raised heart rate, I suppose. But as I've mentioned, my daughter only sprung for the basic model. I don't know if sex would show up as distance traveled or stairs climbed. I guess it would depend, wouldn't it?

Though people of all shapes and sizes wear these things, do we really think they're making any of us fitter, stronger, thinner? And what would our forefathers think? They'd crank out 10,000 steps milking cows and slopping hogs before they even had their first slab of breakfast pie.

But I'm a modern woman. So I'll wear my Fitbit and hope that I'm getting in shape while I dust, make love, or just walk to the wine cellar.

And in 2020, when I win my Olympic gold medal for the 10,000-step track and field event, I will, of course, put my right hand on my heart during the National Anthem. But I'll also raise my left hand so I can verify my steps on my Fitbit.

Kathy —

Put on a happy face!

Risa Nye

Taking My Face Out of the Drawer

by Risa Nye

I used to have a ready-made face. It had natural eyebrows, dark eyelashes, cheeks, (with the soft blush of youth), and rosy lips. My morning ritual was more "grab and go" than a routine of refurbishing with an arsenal of powders and sable brushes. Everything I needed was right there, in front of me, taken for granted and largely ignored.

In my early twenties, I had a friend with the skills of those black-kimono-wearing makeup artists. You know, the women who slink alongside you at the outskirts of the makeup counter, intimating with a raised eyebrow that you could really use what she is hawking.

Now this friend of mine had a "look." On the other hand, I did not have a "look," and, frankly, didn't think I needed one. Until my friend pronounced: "You have great skin. You should be wearing makeup."

What? Wait! *If I have great skin*, I thought, *then why the makeup?* Still, I figured she must know more about the logic of these two things than I do. And I could tell she was regarding me as a project even more than as a friend. People like that, once they're on a mission, it's out of your hands.

I examined her closer and noticed how artistically she had applied the eyeshadow, blush, and mascara that gave her that professional, finished look. Next to her, I felt like a kid in pigtails trying to pass as an adult. *Okay,* I thought, *I'll do it. I'll buy lots of stuff to put on my nice skin to make it look even nicer.*

So one weekend, I went to the nearest Macy's and threw myself on the mercy of the Borghese lady. My friend was with me and this was the line she recommended. I was all in. The Borghese lady was, too. Eager to take a novice under her wing, she may have also sensed a huge commission coming her way.

"She needs everything," my friend announced. With an even bigger grin, the Borghese lady arranged moisturizer, foundation, powder, blush, eyeshadow, brushes, makeup remover, lip gloss, and a few more things that set me back a paycheck or four, neatly in a pile in front of us.

Then (and how she did this I will never know), she managed to fit all of this—my first introduction to the world of big-girl makeup—into a small, clear plastic bag. Now, at last, I would have my very own makeup "routine," that is if I could remember what had just happened and keep it all straight in my head.

My friend nodded her approval, and I felt I had arrived in grown-up land.

Over the next several decades, I waffled between being a stay-at-home mom who may or may not have washed her face three days out of seven, to a graduate student who didn't have time for anything more than a swipe of mascara and some lipstick, to a woman who went to speaking events with the full complement of cover-up, color, and maybe a tiny bit of shimmer when the occasion warranted it. These products were merely enhancements, though. I often skipped a few steps and still felt okay about how I looked.

That was then.

Today, I'm a grandmother and a card-carrying AARPer. And if the truth be told, I have to admit: The face I have these days comes out of my makeup drawer, one hundred percent.

After years of practice and the aid of a 10x

magnifying mirror, I now have that professional put-together look I used to envy in my friend. Every day, I start with a blank canvas. The woman staring back at me hoping for a metamorphosis is my "before" picture. When I'm finished, I look at my "after" self, happy and thankful I've managed to pull off the transformation once again.

When I was a little girl, I was intrigued and mystified hearing women talk about "putting their faces on." I wondered if they could really do that. I stared at them to see if I could tell where their faces attached.

Now, of course, I get it. Although I try not to overdo my makeup, I absolutely must put my face on, or it just doesn't look like "me." Well, maybe the problem is it does look like me, and I'm not ready to accept that...just yet.

A little cover-up for those dark circles, some shaping for those free-range eyebrows, a black mascara that curls as it colors my eyelashes, powder for those spots I just noticed, and a dab of a blush that doesn't look garish for someone my age, and—depending on where I'm going—a hint of eyeshadow that I hope doesn't get lost in the creases, is really all I need.

There I am. That's me.

I've grown accustomed to this face, and if it must come out of the drawer, so be it.

"If you think a minute goes by really fast,
you've never been to a spin class."

—PINTEREST

The Spin Cycle
by Tassie Hewitt Haney

I survived my last birthday, and learned to live with the pile of unwelcome gifts from Mother Nature, including roots that give *Fifty Shades of Gray* new meaning. Some of "Her" presents were as subtle as sweat in the middle of winter, and as tiny as the cluster of smile lines barely visible without reading glasses. She even sent me a greeting card—my very own invitation to membership in AARP.

Yes, "Mom" has blessed me with saddlebags full of cellulite and a healthy dose of absent-mindedness, which I promptly forgot. She also has increased my pluckiness to the point that I sometimes even shock myself by some of the things I say or do.

One episode in particular bears repeating.

"How'd you like to lead the spinning class tomorrow?" the manager of my Fitness Club asked me. "My instructor called in sick and I can't find a sub. "I've seen you take the class, and I'm sure you can fudge it. "Unless it would be too much for you."

"Sure," I said, a bit too quickly. I was flattered beyond words until I thought it through. *You weigh more than you did nine months pregnant,* my inner voice reminded me. *And you'll have to wear spandex...in a mirrored room.*

Somehow, the next day, armed with an iPod of '80s hits and a sense of false bravado, I managed to calm my fears, suck in my stomach, and walk in the spinning room. I smiled confidently at 14 puzzled faces.

A blonde with bee-stung lips in a pumped-up jog bra gave me the once over.

"Where's Veronica?" she asked tartly.

I ignored her. I plugged in my iPod and climbed onto my bike. "I Will Survive" bellowed from the speakers and I pedaled as if what was left of my life depended on it.

A bored-looking young man glanced at his watch. I turned up the volume and pedaled faster. The blonde rolled her eyes. It was then I remembered another advantage of growing older: you don't care what people think anymore. Unless they think you're old.

"What's this? Spinning for Seniors?" the young man wisecracked over the music.

I'll wipe that smirk off his face, I thought. This was war, and it wouldn't end until the blonde's sweat pooled in a puddle at her feet and her boyfriend begged for mercy.

I pedaled faster and faster, cuing the class through standing climbs and jumps. I was a vision in the mirror, a crazed woman with a halo of hair frizzing around my face, one lone gray strand standing defiantly like a diamond-studded exclamation point at the top of my head. My varicose veins pulsed to the beat of the music.

"Sprint!" I demanded. "Faster!" I commanded.

Just then, I noticed a man my age at the back of the class. He met my gaze and smiled, fanning himself with his hand. *At last*, I thought, *some positive feedback*. "Take a Chance on Me" by ABBA blasted from the speakers, and to my surprise, the gentleman pointed to his chest, clearly moved by the words. I felt my face flush and looked away.

It had been several years since my divorce and I had devoted myself completely to my children. This gave me little time to meet new men or date. So I was intrigued. My admirer pantomimed holding a drink, bringing it to his lips suggestively. I glanced away, embarrassed at his attention. His desire was unmistakable. I led the group through a grueling series of jumps, trying to clear my mind.

When it was time for the cool down, I glanced back at my gentleman friend. He winked at me, tugged at his collar, and raised his hand to his mouth, again, in a drinking motion. As the last song came to an end, he hugged the handlebars, clearly a man spent and satisfied, but soon to hunger for more.

The class ended and I smiled triumphantly as I hopped off my bike, gesturing in a fist pump. In my mind I was fantasizing: *We'll meet for drinks. We'll bike off into the sunset. I'll be yours forever, my knight in shining Under Armor.*

I darted to the door.

"Some killer class!" the young man said, trying to catch his breath. I stopped long enough to gloat as the blonde beside him wiped at the sweaty black mascara crying down from her Botoxed brow.

"Hey, but that old dude's barely moving," Blondie said to my back. She was pointing to my would-be suitor. But by then, I was off to the locker room to freshen up quickly, so I could "accidently" bump into my prospective beau on the gym floor.

When I hurried back out, I was deep in thought and missed the wail of the ambulance.

"Where have you been?" the fitness manager screamed at me.

"In the locker room," I answered. "And I have to tell you: I had the best class. Everyone loved me. Well, some more than others, obviously," I said, glancing around for my new friend.

"Never again!" the manager barked. "I knew I was taking a chance, but I never thought it would come to this. Didn't you see that old geezer trying to get your attention? Are you blind?" he screeched, and stalked off to his office.

I clutched my mouth as the paramedics wheeled my ashen admirer out of the spin room. He winced when he saw me and weakly flipped his middle finger, a last defiant gesture.

"The nerve of him," I said to the crowd that gathered. "If he thinks I'm going to nurse him back to health, he's got another think coming."

That was the beginning and the end of my spinning instructor career, as well as my hope of a possible romance.

The good news is that with the help of Mother Nature, it only took a couple of days for my aging mind, with its healthy dose of absent-mindedness, to forget my broken heart. The aches and pains from the spin class took a month.

Only a Coincidence
by Georgia A. Hubley

I must confess I was once a "re-gifter." It started
forty-five years ago, long before an episode of
Seinfeld made "re-gift" a popular word.

Here's how it began. In late October 1963,
I received a teal floral silk scarf for my birthday
from my Aunt Zoe who lived in Florida. The scarf
was a stylish dark cyan color, but it really wasn't
me. I couldn't coordinate it with anything in my
clothes closet. However, I felt guilty about putting
it in some charity donation box.

Then I got a brainstorm. Surely, someone else
might enjoy the scarf. It was brand new, so who'd
be any the wiser? So I set up a "re-gift drawer" in
my bedroom dresser and tucked the scarf away.

Several weeks later, I wrapped the scarf elegantly and gave it to my boss at her birthday luncheon. After cake was served, I watched her open the silver box, slowly, fold back the matching tissue, and carefully lift the scarf to admire it. She smiled, then raised the scarf to her chin and brushed her cheek with the silk fabric.

"It's so soft," she said. "I really like the blue and green in it. It goes so well with my navy blue suit. Thank you so much."

"Glad you like it," I replied, beaming. I felt really smug inside, secretly priding myself for mastering the art of re-gifting.

Thanksgiving was only days away, and I was invited to join my husband and his staff for their annual Thanksgiving potluck. I volunteered to make a pumpkin cheesecake for the occasion.

At noon, I'd arrived with the dessert in hand. As I stood at the front desk waiting for the receptionist to announce my arrival, a delivery man handed her a birthday bouquet. "Thanks!" she squealed. "Oh, giant yellow mums," she said. "They're my favorite."

After retrieving the card clipped to the arrangement, she shared the message with me— the flowers were from her office mates.

"They're really nice to me here," she said. "See, they gave me this box of candy, too, and a gorgeous silk scarf." And with that, she pulled a scarf from a silver box buried beneath other gift boxes stacked on the desk, and draped it around her neck.

I was stunned. It looked like the same silver box, tissue paper, and teal floral silk scarf. *But could it be? Of course not*, I thought. *It's just a coincidence.* I was grateful when my husband appeared a few seconds later and whisked me off to the festivities.

As Christmas neared, I took inventory of my re-gift drawer. I was amazed at the nice things I'd accumulated. There were two bottles of "Tigress Cologne" by Faberge that was all the rage back then, an assortment of trendy gold and silver chunky bracelets, and two simulated pearl necklaces with matching drop earrings. I wrapped each with ribbons and bows, and crossed six people off my Christmas list.

Two weeks before Christmas, I attended my employer's holiday party. Since it was a small financial institution, the affair was an intimate and fun-filled celebration. The highlight was a white elephant gift exchange. The best thing about this type of swap was that everyone got the chance to "steal" or "trade." The gifts ranged from exquisite to outlandish. My contribution was a fondue pot with matching tray and forks.

After we ate, we all pulled a number from a festive green basket. "Let the game begin!" my boss shouted. Since I drew number one, I was the first to choose.

After examining the lot, I picked a package with shiny foil holly wrapping paper. With urging from the others, I untied the red ribbons and ripped open the package.

I was dumbstruck. It was the same silver box tied with silver sequined ribbon. For a moment, I was hopeful. Surely, it was a coincidence. Then, as I unfolded the tissue paper, there was no mistaking the teal floral silk scarf tucked inside. I smiled faintly, and said, "Oh, how lovely."

The fondue set I'd brought was the most popular item stolen and traded. But to my dismay, no one wanted to trade or steal the scarf. At the end of the evening, I wrapped the scarf around my neck, and decided to make one important resolution come the New Year: I would never re-gift again.

On the way home, the low fuel indicator light appeared on the dashboard, and my husband pulled into a gas station. While he filled the tank, I asked the attendant for the bathroom key. Mounted over the toilet was a sign: "Do Not Deposit Feminine Products in the Toilet." There was no warning, however, about flushing silk scarves.

New Year's arrived and the champagne flowed freely at our neighborhood's holiday party.

At the stroke of midnight, I toasted with my husband and four of our closest friends. Everyone took turns revealing their resolutions. I waited until last. I just couldn't tell them about the scarf incident.

"I don't believe in making New Year's resolutions," I lied. "Besides, who keeps them anyway?"

I have never told a soul about that phantom scarf's demise...until now...or that I made the decision to never re-gift again. Actually, it is the only New Year's resolution I have ever kept.

The traveling scarf may have been a coincidence. But, just in case, I'm not taking any chances.

"Love is a lot like a backache: it doesn't show up on
X-rays, but you know it's there."
—GEORGE BURNS

Love Is More than a Bottle of 'Heavenly Nights' and a Diamond Journey Necklace

by Allia Zobel Nolan

For as long as I can remember, there has been a notion "out there" suggesting the amount of happiness and fulfillment in a woman's relationship is directly related to the amount of goo-goo-eyed, hearts-and-flowers, Tiffany— not Overstock—diamond-jewelry romance she experiences.

This idea seems to permeate everything—TV, videos, bodice-rippers, women's magazines, movies, not to mention any number of advertisements from hair dye to teeth whitener.

If we can accept everything we see and read, this "romance quotient" is measured in certain quantifiable, demonstrative displays—such as how many times our boyfriend/husband/significant other wines and dines us (with candles and minimum $24.99 bottle of Merlot) and how much and how often he compliments us and professes his undying love.

Romance is also, if we can believe the ads, measured in the amount of consistently bought (impromptu or under pressure) gifts the lover showers upon the woman, high among which are special-order salted caramel chocolates from Godiva (a Whitman Sampler in a pinch); expensive fragrances with names like "Longing," "Seductive," and "Jump Me;" lots of gold trinkets; anything from Victoria's Secret; dozens of long-stemmed yellow (red is out this year) roses; and at least one impulse romantic getaway trip to a Caribbean island, or if money is tight, a weekend in Amish Country, or if it's really tight, a visit to the Bronx Zoo.

If any of this is missing, we are led to believe the romance is finis, because the man is either taking the woman for granted, bored to tears, or just plain doesn't love her anymore. (Naturally, it's the woman's fault. She walked around too often in her fleece pj bottoms, university sweats, and Uggs.)

In any event, since romance is reportedly the glue that keeps relationships from falling apart, then it is only a matter of time before the man will take off in search of this illusive—but must-have—key to happiness and look for it in the arms of another woman, a woman of mystery and sultry eyelids, who'll wait in a steamy Casablanca-like bar, e-cigarette in one hand, organic wine in the other, ready to kiss and snuggle for hours after which the two will steal away to the South of France to live adrift in an I-can't-live-without-you, lovely-dovey romantic stupor.

This is a dangerous notion. It's what, I believe, is responsible for a great deal of unhappiness and an even greater number of divorces.

It's also what I believe keeps a lot of women (and men, too) unsatisfied, searching for that amorous nirvana—a fantasy bubble of perfect bliss which the world popularizes as totally achievable—under the right circumstances.

The purveyors of gibberish like this really do women a great disservice. They want us to believe that romance is the same thing as love, that there is no love if you don't have romance, and that the romance a woman does have should be equal to or more than her neighbor's, and as electric as the day she and her partner first nibbled each other's earlobes.

As most of us know or (hopefully) come to learn, this is pure rubbish. Though romance is nifty, it's not the be all and end all of a relationship. And, as the song bemoans, if your man doesn't "bring flowers" anymore, so what? He pays the mortgage or does nice things like empty the dishwasher, or offers to take the kids to the mall, or the cats to the vet, so you'll have time to write your blog or soak in a hot bath, actions, which—while they may not categorically be considered romantic—are just as meaningful a sign of love as any diamond and ruby drop earrings.

Now, I don't have a daughter, unless you count the furry one with four legs on the back of my chair. But if I did, I'd teach her to separate love and romance as soon as she stopped crawling. To help her clear up the difference, I'd give her my own definitions of each.

Love, I'd tell her, is a permanent, real-life, enduring, reality-based bond. It doesn't need Tiffany bracelets or oyster and champagne dinners to survive. Love allows partners to cherish each other—warts and all—while they face good and not-so-good times, as well as challenges like house alterations, kids, cats, unemployment, death, the effects of gravity on the body, depletion of funds, hormones, Presidential races, cesspool backups, hair transplants, aging, and the like.

On the other hand, romance, I'd say—though thoroughly delightful and enchanting—is ever-so-fleeting, thrives on rose-colored glasses, and calls to mind the stuff of fairy tales. In fact, I'd tell her, romance is a lot like expensive perfume—it's intense at first, but it evaporates much too soon.

To: Kathy, you are a goddess, and I'm so glad to be your friend. BIG hugs! Christy Heitger-Ewing XO

"Beauty begins the moment you decide to be yourself."
—COCO CHANEL

You've Been Doing It All Wrong

by Christy Heitger-Ewing

I was channel surfing the other day when I came across a *Dr. Oz Show* that caught my attention. The segment was called "Beauty Secrets Debunked." I stayed tuned because I thought I might learn a thing or two, and I did. But boy, was my education depressing.

For example, did you know that plucking a gray hair from your head damages the follicles so severely that hair may not grow back there at all? And if it does, not only will the hair still grow back gray, but it will also sprout in the opposite direction as the rest of your hair, making the gray even more noticeable?

I look back on all the hours I've spent, cross-eyed, leaning close to the bathroom mirror, plucking away at those stray grays. And to think, I've been hastening the balding process, pluck by pluck.

In addition to my eager tweezing, I've been sleeping on my side for decades now—ever since my OBGYN told me it was the best thing for pregnancy. Now Dr. Oz says that side-sleeping causes delicate facial skin to wrinkle. Well, drat! The OBGYN could have at least warned me.

I'll spare you the sagging breast question Dr. Oz fielded from an audience member. Suffice it to say that the makeshift model he used to demonstrate the way in which nursing a baby and the mere passage of time impact breast tissue was nothing short of horrifying. I cringed and cupped my breasts in the same way a man reflexively grabs his privates each time he watches a video of a crotch hit.

Anyone who proclaims that age is nothing more than a number has not yet begun to physically fall apart. For me, random ailments started plaguing me several years ago—nothing that would be considered a medical disaster, but highly aggravating nonetheless. For example, I used to ride in the car for long distances without any problem. Then one summer, I exited the passenger's side of my Toyota 4-Runner after a long stretch and noticed my back was insanely stiff. I shrugged it off, assuming the feeling would subside. But, instead, I battled chronic back pain for several months. And this just from riding in a car.

Another time I hopped off the back of a boat's swim platform into waist-deep water. This was merely a baby hop, mind you—onto a sand-bottom lake, no less. It should have been no biggie. But when my heel hit the lake's bottom, a piercing pain shot through my right foot. Afterwards, nagging plantar fasciitis plagued me for over six months.

I've also suffered from tennis elbow despite the fact that I never play tennis. Doctors say this injury came about because I sleep curled on my side (as evidenced by my wrinkly face) with my right arm tucked beneath me. Bending the arm is apparently a ligament no-no; it's better to sleep with the arm outstretched, especially when a tendon is inflamed. Boy, do I miss the days when I could conk out, willy-nilly, and wake up feeling rested instead of wounded.

Honestly, I think all of these irritating injuries are karma for the ribbing I gave my grandparents when I was a kid.

"What do you mean you don't want to ride the roller coaster?" I'd ask Grandma and Grandpa. "It's not that bumpy!" I insisted. (Meanwhile, the wooden death machine whipped around the tracks so violently that my earrings would pop out.)

Then, too, every time my grandparents came for a visit, within an hour of arrival, they made a beeline for our sofa. "You just got here. You're seriously going to take a nap?" I'd ask with disgust. As a youngster, I could not, for the life of me, understand the appeal of catching Zzzs during daylight hours. Now, of course, I start to salivate if I know I've a shot at 15 minutes of shut-eye even if I've just gotten up.

My grandparents knew a good thing when they saw it—an empty couch, for instance. And that's not all. I remember Grandma used to go on and on about how lovely I was. In fact, she often told me, "You're so pretty, you'd look good with a burlap bag over your head." It sounded like a backhanded compliment at the time.

Today, what with the wrinkles and wily stray gray popping up here and there, the burlap bag doesn't sound like a half-bad suggestion.

Still, with age comes wisdom, and now I understand the meaning of Grandma's message. I look back at my teenage pictures and realize I actually was a hottie! But I never thought so at the time. I only focused on the zit, or the freckle, or the number on the scale. I didn't appreciate what I had when I had it. Now that I'm older, my perspective has shifted. I recognize that the "here and now" all too quickly becomes the "there and then."

Grandma encouraged me to embrace my beauty, brains, health, and wellness (just as Dr. Oz has encouraged me to embrace the invention of the support bra). So these days, I let the chips fall where they may and the hairs grow where they gray.

And that's my beauty secret, debunked.

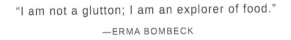

"I am not a glutton; I am an explorer of food."

—ERMA BOMBECK

Scaling the Weight Wall

by Sharon M. Kennedy

In 1977, I was as slim and trim as any other 30-year-old divorcée in Michigan. I worked for a law firm in downtown Detroit. My respectable job required sensible suits and dresses, so I pushed my free-flowing maxi skirts, tie-dyed T-shirts, and skin-tight, size-five Gloria Vanderbilt jeans to the back of my closet. They reappeared on the weekend, along with my cowboy boots, outback-style Aussie hat, striped shirt, and denim vest.

When I look at photographs from that time, I marvel at how thin and stylish I was. I never dreamed I'd morph into an overweight, 70-year-old woman.

I thought I'd always be thin. It never occurred

to me something incredibly strange would happen when I turned 65. Nobody warned me I would slam into the weight wall like a hockey player hitting the boards. One day I was slim. The next day nothing fit.

In my confused state, I went to the doctor, certain I had stomach tumors. When tests came back negative, I convinced myself I had celiac disease. A trip to the health food store saw me stocking up on all the gluten-free products I could find. I was sure my basket of expensive flours, seeds, and non-GMO items would solve my phenomenal weight gain.

I returned home eager to bake a batch of sorghum cookies and a loaf of buckwheat bread. When they came out of the oven, I happily consumed them...and was thoroughly disappointed. Wheat was clearly not the culprit. I could tolerate gluten as well as most people. So something else must have been responsible, for sure.

Undaunted, I figured I was retaining fluids. So I made a trip to Walmart. I spent an hour reading the labels of every remedy for water retention. I purchased a variety of pills guaranteed to shed all extra liquid from my body. After a few days, I realized the pills were as useless as feathers on a dog's back.

Finally, I had to admit the truth. I was fat. There was no way around it. I know the "f" word is politically incorrect. But, when you're fat, you're fat. And there's no point in trying to pretend otherwise. My metabolism had quit on me, had simply given up, while my dining habits had remained the same.

An awful depression shrouded me until my brother, Ed, came to my rescue. He told me about the amazing "Rock Diet." He said it was fairly new to the market and hadn't been tested on too many rats. But he assured me it was guaranteed to work. Available research was scant, but I listened intently as Ed explained it was worth a try. After all, he said, I had nothing to lose except some extra pounds.

The Rock Diet was simple. All I had to do was carry a rock and I would lose weight. Whenever I reached for a Snickers bar or a bag of chips, I could hold the rock in my hand and it would prevent me from snacking. Along with a sensible diet and plenty of exercise, the Rock Diet was a modern miracle, my brother promised. He said most people had never heard of it because it hadn't gotten rave reviews on the *Dr. Oz Show*.

Well, I figured if one rock was good, two were better. So I went outside and found the prettiest ones I could find on the ground. I put one in my purse and one in my pocket. Then I went to town.

My first stop was Dairy Queen. As I enjoyed my hot fudge sundae, I wondered why my rocks didn't make me feel guilty. I decided ice cream must be okay. I swirled the delicious cold vanilla into a sea of thick, rich fudge sauce and heaps of salted peanuts. Oh, the delight of ice cream on a warm summer day thrilled me. Even better was the knowledge that the Rock Diet allowed such a pleasure. A shudder of sheer satisfaction pulsed through me.

When I finished my scrumptious treat, my next stop was Arby's and some curly fries. *Surely the Rock Diet will kick in now*, I thought. But as I doused the tasty fries with a generous helping of ketchup, my rocks remained silent.

I had one more stop to test the validity of the diet. I headed for Domino's and a thin-crust pizza loaded with pepperoni and cheese. We all know thin crust is like eating soda crackers, and *they* certainly have no calories. I sat in my car and munched away while my rocks were as mute as a mime. Regardless of what I consumed, it went like that for the rest of the month. My Rock Diet was a total failure.

So here I am, five years later, still overweight, and still unwilling to admit defeat. I'm sure the diet just needs some little adjustment. So I'll continue carrying these rocks with me until I can squeeze into my Vanderbilts, hip-huggers, and maybe even my hoard of miniskirts—the ones I found under the pile of size 2X, elastic-waisted, baggy fleece pants.

I did think about giving away the clothes and be done with it. But I'm not a quitter. Hope does, indeed, spring eternal in my heart.

Maybe I just need to carry heavier rocks.

The Pierced
by Allia Zobel Nolan

Mention body piercing and the first thing I think of, after an initial involuntary flinch, is the good guy in a ghoulie movie running a stake through a vampire to persuade him to stay dead.

Well, nowadays, everyone knows you don't have to be a vampire to get yourself perforated. Fact is, ordinary men and women (I called them "The Pierced") are getting more holes drilled in them than there are in a packet of imported Swiss cheese. It's a fad I can sum up in two words: "Ouch," and *"Ewwww!"*

And we're not just talking ears here. Though that's a good place to start. Today, real men—from news anchors to corporate types—wear one if not more studs in their lobes. Those with panache don matching sets of kissing dolphins. And it's not uncommon to tune in the TV to see a linebacker in shoulder pads and greasepaint sporting a pair of gold hoops that starlets who walk the Red Carpet would salivate over.

But that's not the half of it. The Pierced distribute the wealth evenly. So you'll notice studs, rings, and chains all over their bodies—in their noses, fingers, chins, nipples, belly buttons and/or other places only their significant others can admire. Experts who study stuff like this (yes, there really are such people) say it's a way for man to get in touch with his primitive self. Either that or he's watching too many pirate movies.

Okay, men are from Mars, anyway. What's women's excuse? Theorists claim women are spiking themselves silly for various reasons: Some for shock value. Some because they want to be different. Some to cover up hurt and confusion.

I think it's the jewelry they're after. Women recognize an opportunity when they see one. They realize the more places you have to wear jewelry, the more jewelry you can expect. To them, piercing equals an increase in resources. It means goodbye tiny velvet box with two pearl studs; hello treasure chest of diamonds, sapphires, and rubies.

I, myself, wouldn't lance anything I didn't have to for all the baubles in Beyoncé's safety deposit box. But then every generation has its off-the-wall fads. And in fact, far from being a troublemaker, one of The Pierced has actually turned out my helpmate. See, I used to have trouble resisting dessert at my favorite lunch spot. But now that a waitress there has pierced her brow, nose, and lip, all I need do is glance her way, and, *zap*, my chocolate mousse craving passes.

I have to hand it to The Pierced. Their individuality's not just idle talk. It comes with pain, danger, and a heap of challenge. For instance, I can't imagine what it would be like talking with a studded tongue. People already say I sound like I have a mouth full of marbles. Would a tongue stud make things better or worse?

What about eating? If I had ice cream for lunch, would my studs stay freezing until dinner? Likewise, if I had coffee McDonald's-hot, would the rings in my mouth conduct the heat and scald me? Spinach stuck in my studs would be embarrassing. But maybe in time, eateries would offer stud picks right there next to toothpicks.

At the airport, would I have to stand to the side and remove my hardware before I went through security so I wouldn't trigger the alarms?

When it came to romance, could I deal with getting my tongue tangled, my nose locked, or my body entwined in other, more intimate places?

And on the job, could I deal with the squeamish

Unpierced who might complain to the boss and insist on a "non-body pierced environment" desk far from me?

These are quandaries I'll never have to face since I prefer my jewelry pinned on me not through me. As for The Pierced, who am I to judge? If they want to puncture their parts, far be it from me to needle them.

A Salute to Erma

> "When I stand before God at the end of my life,
> I would hope that I don't have a single bit
> of talent left and could say, 'I used everything
> you gave me.'"
>
> —ERMA BOMBECK

Erma Bombeck: Laughing Through the Pain

by Allia Zobel Nolan

Most people have a hero. Someone they admire. Mine was Erma Bombeck. She did more for the American housewife than any other woman. She validated her and gave her a voice. For starters, she admitted she was one. Then she went on to build a career around writing about what it was like.

Bombeck was to housewives what Spock was to babies. We grew up reading her. Her material came from her own experiences. She held up a mirror to her life, burst out laughing, then sat down and chronicled it for millions to enjoy.

And boy, did we ever. We devoured each word of her columns, then excised them neatly with coupon cutters to pass along to a friend or hang prominently on the refrigerator door, under the cow magnet.

That's because Bombeck was "Everywoman." We were her; she was us. When she wrote about her adventures in "ma-ma" land, we roared, because they were our adventures. We could relate to dust bunnies under the bed so thick they clogged the Hoovers. We had served not-quite-defrosted white bread and Spaghetti-O's (with ketchup) for dinner (on occasion). And we could recognize what a sardine sandwich smelled like after a month in a jeans' back pocket. We could identify with tile fungus. We knew from husbands who snored. We had experience with neighbors' dogs that pooped in our yards.

Indeed, *Woman's Day* and *Good Housekeeping* gave us the ideal. But Bombeck gave us the truth. She was the first woman to hint that being a housewife might/just/could, possibly not be all it's cracked up to be. Still, because she wrote about it with such hilarity and absence of malice, it was okay. So what if it were more fake geraniums than long-stemmed roses; more *Barney Goes to the Zoo* than Martha Stewart moments? Every profession had its ups and downs. Truth is, the inanities of being a housewife were, for Bombeck, what made it such a hoot.

Bombeck was first to go public with the idea that housewives didn't have to be perfect. She dispelled the myth of "the total woman" as just that: a fairy tale perpetrated by the same folks who brought us girdles and *The Stepford Wives*. And if you burnt the roast or hemmed your husband's pants with a stapler, you weren't odd. You were normal.

Bombeck made it okay not to look like a Barbie doll, cook like The Galloping Gourmet and keep house like Mr. Clean. In fact, if you managed to change the beds and shave your legs once a month, you were doing just fine. Indeed, and if you didn't have a religious experience when you diapered the baby, you weren't strange. She never said you had to love putting down toilet seats and cleaning chrome fixtures with a toothbrush, just that since you were going to do it anyway, why not have fun with it? She certainly did.

Bombeck not only raised the status of women as housewives and moms, she also put "women's humor" on the map. With her successes, (syndication in 900 papers at the height of her popularity and 12 books, nine of which made *The New York Times* bestseller list), she legitimized women's humor as relevant commentary, no longer relegated to an occasional essay on the back page. Not surprisingly, she paved the way for zillions of Bombeck wannabees to be taken seriously.

What makes Bombeck even more remarkable is she did this under enormous hardship. She suffered kidney disease, which eventually led to a three-times-a-day dialysis. On top of that, she developed breast cancer and had to have a mastectomy.

Through it all, she kept her spirits up and her writing jovial. "(So) I wrote all these books with a kidney problem," she told an interviewer once. "That doesn't affect your brain. It doesn't affect your sense of humor."

Thank goodness for us. Still, Bombeck was never the type to complain. She preferred to count her blessings, not her ills. When something bad came her way, she smoothed down her apron, and did what any good housewife would do: got on with things. But then, what else would you expect from someone who listed her hobby as "dust?"

Golly, I miss her.

And The Writers Are...

Amy McVay Abbott

Amy McVay Abbott, an Indiana author who writes about healthcare and humor, has penned four books, including *Whitley County Kid*. Retired from a 35-year career, Abbott knows humor and health are more connected than they appear. Find her online at *www.amyabbottwrites.com* and read her blog, The Raven Lunatic.

Elaine Ambrose

Elaine Ambrose is a bestselling author of eight books, including *Midlife Happy Hour,* which *Publishers Weekly* reviewed as "laugh-out-loud funny!" She's an internationally known blogger, humorous speaker, workshop facilitator, and community volunteer. Find her books and events on *www.elaineambrose.com*.

Karen G. Anderson

Karen G. Anderson works and gardens in Seattle. She's a freelance writer whose career has spanned newspaper reporting, crime fiction reviewing, science fiction, content management for the iTunes Music Store, and humor columns. She lives with her partner, The Scholarly Gentleman, and an undisclosed number of cats.

Karla Araujo

Karla Araujo has never been at a loss for words. She's written everything from children's coloring books to the text for Triscuit boxes, magazine features, ad campaigns, and personal essays. Araujo lives in Naples, Florida, where she teaches creative writing and plays entirely too much tennis.

Leslie Bamford

Leslie Bamford came of age in the 1960s in Montreal, Quebec. Retired, she lives in Waterloo, Ontario, where she enjoys writing in several genres, when she isn't outside in extreme Canadian weather, trying to keep up with her energetic husband and a quirky dog.

Tracy Roberts Buckner

Tracy Roberts Buckner contributes to the *Observer Tribune* family of newspapers and blogs for the Erma Bombeck Writers' Workshop. She enjoys writing about life's slow decline and vows to go down kicking and screaming. Follow her at Aging, Kids, and Why We Self-Medicate at *www.tracybuckner.com.*

Jennifer Byrne

Among other places, Jennifer Byrne's writing has appeared in *The New Yorker* Daily Shouts & Murmurs, The *Huffington Post*, *McSweeney's.net*, *The Hairpin*, and *The Second City Network*. She lives in New Jersey with her husband and her two children, who cough up hairballs and walk on four feet instead of two.

Michelle Poston Combs

Michelle Poston Combs writes humorous and serious observations on life, menopause, anxiety, and marriage on her site, Rubber Soles in Hell at *www.rubbershoesinhell.com*.

Kaye Curren

Kaye Curren is a retired event planner. She has returned to writing after 30 years raising two husbands, two children, two teenage stepchildren, three horses, umpteen dogs and cats, and several non-speaking parakeets. Find her work on her website/blog at *www.writethatthang.com.*

Fritzy Dean

Fritzy Dean is an 82-year-old mother, grandmother, and great grandmother who fell in love with words at an early age. She has been published in community newspapers and magazines. But the accomplishment she is proudest of is opening up the world of books to little readers as a hometown reading volunteer.

Lori B. Duff

Lori B. Duff is a recovering lawyer, and an unrepentant proponent of the Oxford comma and the two-spaces-after-a-period rule. Her latest book is *Mismatched Shoes and Upside Down Pizza.* You can find her other award-winning books, her blog, and some other drivel at *www.loriduffwrites.com.*

Janene Dutt

Janene Dutt resides on a small island in the Pacific Northwest with her family. Recently, her three children asked her 159 questions in six hours. When she's not being interrogated, you can find her blogging about family life at *www.imightbefunny.com*.

Cindy Eastman

Cindy Eastman is an award-winning author, educator, workshop leader, and homebody. She's the author of *Flip-Flops after 50: And Other Thoughts on Aging I Remembered to Write Down.* Eastman is currently working on her next book, which will continue to look at aging though the lens of wit and humor.

Janie Emaus

Janie Emaus believes when the world is falling apart, we're just one laugh away from putting it back together. She is the author of the novel, *Mercury in Retro Love*, and hundreds of short stories, essays, and blogs. To read more about Janie, please visit her website *www.Janieemaus.com*.

Christy Heitger-Ewing

Christy Heitger-Ewing, an award-winning writer who pens human interest stories for national, regional, and local magazines, has contributed to 18 anthologies; is the author of *Cabin Glory: Amusing Tales of Time Spent at the Family Retreat, www.cabinglory.com*; and lives in Indiana with her husband, two sons, and two cats.

Bonnie Jean Feldkamp

Bonnie Jean Feldkamp is an award-winning blogger for *Cincinnati Family Magazine* and the Communications Director for the National Society of Newspaper Columnists. She has written for *The New York Times*, *Child Magazine,* and more. Find her on social media *@WriterBonnie* or at *www.WriterBonnie.com*.

Sharon Gerger

Sharon Gerger is an award-winning writer with work published in *The New Yorker, Glimmer Train, Harper's*. Okay, so that's all balderdash. She writes a lot and sometimes people publish her work and that fills her with bliss. If they happen to pay her, well, good-gosh-galoshes, she gets sort of delirious.

Tassie Hewitt Haney

Tassie Hewitt Haney is a Houston-based freelance writer, graduate of Texas Christian University, and mother of three. She spends her days collecting embarrassing moments and her nights writing, changing names to protect the guilty. Find her at *www.TassieWriteNow.wordpress.com*.

Georgia A. Hubley

Georgia A. Hubley retired from the money world after 20 years to write about her world. Vignettes of her life appear in scores of various anthologies, magazines, and newspapers. Learn more at her website: *www.georgiahubley.com*

Carolyn Anderson Jones

Carolyn Anderson Jones, an Indie writer, free spirit, and lover of animals, has four published novels (*www.carolynandersonjones.com/books*), three of which are set in her home state, beautiful Colorado. When not writing, she can be found kayaking and hiking, or spending time with her kids and grandkids.

Sharon M. Kennedy

Sharon M. Kennedy, a newspaper columnist who lives in a mobile home on a quiet country road in Michigan, published her first book, *Life in a Tin Can,* in 2016. Her philosophy is simple: Vick's VapoRub is the answer to all life's problems. She has aged gracefully, but proudly admits: "I don't live with a dozen cats."

Sherri Kuhn

Sherri Kuhn's writing has been featured in *The Washington Post, Today Parenting, Mom.me,* and *SheKnows.* She was a cast member in the 2012 "Listen to Your Mother" show and lives in Northern California in her mostly empty nest with her husband and crazy yellow lab.

Sandy Lingo

Sandy Lingo's mother and grandmother read Erma's columns to her, and Erma's humor left its imprint. Lingo is a mother and a retired middle school teacher, so she has plenty of laughable material to mine. Her blog, A Second Helping, can be found at *www.sandylingo.com*.

Lisa Marlin

Lisa Marlin's essays have appeared on the Erma Bombeck Writers' Workshop blog and in *Writer's Digest Magazine*, *Dallas Morning News*, and *The Denver Post*. Going on 30 years, her four children continue to be her greatest source of joy, worry, and writing prompts. She posts at *www.lisamarlin.com*.

Kelly L. McKenzie

Quirk magnet Kelly L. McKenzie hopes to age as well as her 95-year-old mom whom she often writes about on her blog Just TypiKel. Readers finally spurred McKenzie to write a memoir about the ten years they survived working together selling Asian antiques. Her mother eagerly awaits its completion.

Amy Mullis

Amy Mullis lives in upstate South Carolina. She can no longer wear hot pants, but the memories still fit just fine. Her work has appeared in newspapers, magazines, online, and in various flavors of anthologies. She took Honorable Mention honors in the 2010 Erma Bombeck Writing Competition.

Alice Muschany

Alice Muschany writes about everyday life with a touch of humor. Her essays have been published in *Guideposts* as well as *Cup of Comfort, Chicken Soup for the Soul, Not Your Mother's Book,* and Gloria Gaynor's *We Will Survive* anthology.

Allia Zobel Nolan

Allia Zobel Nolan is an internationally published author of 175+ children's and adult books, which reflect her two main passions, God and cats, and include among others, *Whatever Is Lovely, Cat Confessions, Women Who Still Love Cats Too Much, The Worrywart's Prayer Book,* and *Angels in the Bible Storybook.* Find her at ***www.AlliaWrites.com***.

Risa Nye

Risa Nye's work has appeared in various national publications and anthologies. Her memoir, *There Was a Fire Here,* was published in 2016. Nye also writes about cocktails under the name of Ms. Barstool for *Berkeleyside.* Find out more at ***www.risanye.com***. She lives in California; at last count, she has five grandchildren.

Anne Elise O'Connor

Anne Elise O'Connor is an Emmy award-winning writer, a survivor of heart disease, internet dating, cancer, and a divorce. She has an alter-ego named Dramatica, who may be prettier and younger. But as she can be deleted with the push of a button, Anne Elise is boss. Find them at *www.DramaticaDealsWith.com*.

Lucia Paul

Lucia Paul is an award-winning humor writer whose work has been included in numerous anthologies, including *That's Paris: Life, Love and Sarcasm in the City of Light, Motherhood May Cause Drowsiness—Stories by Sleepy Moms,* and *It's Really 10 Months—Special Delivery.*

Yvonne Ransel

Yvonne Ransel is a writer of essays—some humorous, some poignant—who is inspired by life's crazy everyday events. She was a librarian, then a bar owner, and now a librarian again. She survived the '60s, the millennium, and the years since, as wife, mother, and grandmother of six.

Lorraine Ray

Lorraine Ray is the author of the devotional *Yes, Cheese-Us Loves Me!* She is an associate professor emeritus at Ohio University and a preschool music teacher and founder-director of Aiken Kinderchoir in South Carolina. Ray is also the proud mom of Michael (Danielle) and two adorable grandchildren.

Joanne Salemink

Joanne Salemink is a recovering journalist and former high school teacher. She routinely embarrasses her family and friends by blogging about them at *www.Sandwichmomonwry.blogspot.com*. She recently self-published a humorous novel, *Scout's Honor*, and is threatening to write more.

Amy Hartl Sherman

Amy Hartl Sherman is a writer, cartoonist, humorist, and retired flight attendant. The latter inspired the former. She raised two sons and one husband in Glen Ellyn, Illinois. She's the creator and curator of *www.krankykitty.com* and *www.facebook.com/AmyHartlSherman*.

Barbara L. Smith

Barbara L. Smith wrote a humor column for a local paper for nearly ten years. She is also an award-winning playwright whose play "Butterscotch" was published by Samuel French, produced around the country, and optioned for a TV movie. Her latest play is "Lotsa Pluck: Surviving Death and Second-Hand Smoke."

DC Stanfa

DC Stanfa is the author of *The Art of Table Dancing: Escapades of an Irreverent Woman* and co-editor of *Fifty Shades of Funny: Hook-ups, Break-ups, and Crack-ups.* She's an expert on fun and its by-product, trouble. Armed with sarcasm and a pen, she proves truth is funnier than fiction.

Sherry Stanfa-Stanley

Sherry Stanfa-Stanley is the author of *Finding My Badass Self: A Year of Truths and Dares,* which chronicles her misadventures embarking on an "un-bucket list." Her writing appears in *The Rumpus, Healthy Aging, First for Women,* and the anthology *Fifty Shades of Funny.* Read more at *www.sherrystanfa-stanley.com.*

Janine V. Talbot

Janine V. Talbot googled "I want to be Erma Bombeck" four years ago and everything changed. A proud mom of two daughters, she resides in southern Maine with her spouse and two-and-a-half cats. Her column appears in two Maine papers, and she received an award from the National Society of Newspaper Columnists.

Denise Denton Thiery

Denise Denton Thiery grew up in a home in which a sense of humor was highly valued and often practiced by a mother with lightning-quick wit that leaned toward the risqué and a father who was the master of convoluted wordplay. She learned very early the rewards of making others laugh.

Pamela Wright

Pamela Wright is an award-winning essayist and humor writer. She lives in Clarkdale, Georgia, with the world's most adorable mutt and two cats named Zelda and Gracie, affectionately known as The Old Maid Starter Kit. Her essay, "Sweating Bullets," originally appeared on *Purple Clover*.

About the Erma Bombeck Writers' Workshop

The Erma Bombeck Writers' Workshop has been dubbed the "Woodstock of Humor."

The University of Dayton held the first workshop in 2000 as a one-time event to commemorate the Bombeck family's gift of Erma's papers to her alma mater. Erma's famous friends—columnist Art Buchwald, "Family Circus" cartoonist Bil Keane, and author and ERA advocate Liz Carpenter—headlined the event. The workshop was so successful—and so much fun—that the university decided to continue it, reconvening every other year. Immensely popular, it sells out within hours.

The workshop's mission is simple: to encourage and inspire writers in the same way Erma found encouragement and inspiration at the University of Dayton. Its mantra is timeless: "You can write!"

Every writer has a book in her. This book grew out of that belief.

–Teri Rizvi, Founder and Director,
Erma Bombeck Writers' Workshop